Digital Transformation – Industry 4.0

Strategize your Digital Transformation Projects

■ ■ ■

Jayaraman KALAIMANI &

Prashant KUMAR

Digital Transformation – Industry 4.0: How to strategize your Digital Transformation Projects

Copyright © 2018 by Jayaraman KALAIMANI

We would like to dedicate this book to our friends, family & Guru, Swami Vivekananda, Maharishi Vethathiri.

Authors:

Jay, KALAIMANI

(Prolific author & Spiritualist)

Author of the bestselling book:
SAP Project Management Pitfalls -
Published by Apress, New York, USA

&

Prashant, KUMAR

(Co-author, M.S., EGMP-IIM, Bangalore)
IIM, Bangalore Alumni

Table of Contents

Foreword

In today's increasingly digital world, every Organization is striving towards the digital transformation with the focus of enhancing customer value proposition and operating model with new avenues of revenues generated.

The one, who is able to embrace the change towards Digital Transformation journey, will survive through the difficult market conditions. The Digital initiatives may sound disruptive in the beginning, with the return on investments (ROI) achieved over a period of time. It is imperative for the businesses to re-think the strategies towards Digital Transformation. As an example, for the honorary Prime Minister of India, Mr. Narendra Modi, who has led the world's largest democratic country towards the Digital transformation initiatives, thus leading by example! Today, India is driving towards smart cities with over $150 Billion USD planned over next couple of decades.

'Digital Transformation - Industry 4.0' book has arrived at the right time when the change is imminent. I am sure readers will find it interesting to read through the case studies and the Digital Transformation strategies succinctly discussed in this book.

Prashant, KUMAR
Digital Transformation Leader
India.

Acknowledgments

Our deepest heartfelt thanks to the incredible work by Amazon KDP press, who is our publisher. It was a journey of the breakthrough in technology and the Digital Transformation strategies are still evolving as a way forward to conduct business in every part of the world.

We would like to thank our colleagues for supporting us through the endeavor. A book of this magnitude would not have been possible without the support of them all. Our sincere thanks to the team for proofreading throughout the stages of this book.

Our sincere thanks to all our friends and families for encouraging us through this digital journey and inspiring us through the ordeal. Our special thanks to Goutam, WURITI for his enthusiasm and proof-read support for this project.

Above all thanking the Divine Space in each of us, thank you—for everything. We have compiled this book based to help you gain insights into the Digital Transformation strategies and start the journey we are all on right now. And we look forward to an eventful 2018.

Introduction

The Digital evolution is not a myth! It is a reality. Industries have transformed from a rugged looking shop-floor to the state-of-the-art facilities. It encompasses the gamut of technologies ranging from mobility, robotics, sensors, big data, analytics, Industrial Internet of Things (IIoT), Artificial Intelligence (AI), Virtual Reality (VR), mechatronics, cyber-security and cloud computing in so-called 3rd technology platform. It's no longer a lame shop-floor with machines churning in and out as you'd imagine.

Perhaps, every machine will be packaged with sensors, IoT device capabilities to transmit data back and forth to process information enabled via Wi-Fi. These are known as smart machines. These smart factories are evolving with the capacity to be completely autonomous and take appropriate actions. Thus, industrial machines will be transcended into intelligent machines that are capable of thinking beyond human imagination as these cognitive systems are evolving. It will continue to transform Industries to be completely autonomous and not just automating processes. It's not a sci-fi movie; it's real and the transformation is happening here and now.

We did witness the transformation in Oct 2017 at SAP TechEd. This event was a confluence of Digital Transformation technocrats discussing various topics. Each topic was focused towards Digital Transformation. The topic of transformation was the most important theme of the world largest software provider, SAP, which has transcended from a technology-oriented approach to the business-oriented approach. Thus, focusing on user experience, design-thinking approach, and flexibility in adapting to the business requirements with an innovative mindset

Based on the recent innovative approach, forklifts in the factories have changed from just being mechanical in supporting operations to the intelligent machines that can transmit information back and forth in off-loading packages in the warehouse using sensors enabled devices with the machine learning can adapt to the environment. The RFID tags can notify the inventory movements and further process data via machine learning capabilities to empower machines to become autonomous over a period.

Is this a real challenge to the survival of the human work-force? Or is this a pursuit of achieving operational excellence? Perhaps these machines can become the smart executives at some point with the enormous data and AI capabilities, which means, these machines can think and act as you do. Did you know the World Best Chess champion Mr.Gary Kasparov lost to the autonomous chess algorithm system? This was the first step in machine winning over humans. It was demonstrated by IBM Watson, a humungous system with Artificial Intelligence (AI) capabilities. IBM has invested in 'AI' platform in every sector to achieve operational excellence with completely autonomous capabilities. Just imagine the autonomous AI systems that can collect data, process it and transform it to outcome-based benefits to the business.

The traditional database (dB) systems, IT Infrastructure, software applications landscape is changing; as we see the transformation from the on-premises solution to the Cloud-based solution, with no upfront capital expenditure (CAPEX) to the subscription model. This change will provide benefits to the customers to spend quality time in innovation and new product design innovation (NPI) and development without worrying about the day-to-day operational issues. Further deep into consumable services model with an open source platform that can be customized to the customer bespoke requirements; today, customer behavior has changed and they want more flexible solutions. The customer wants it real-time, right away with the ability to process data real-time.

This will necessitate organization quickly analyze, build intelligence by slicing and dicing data real-time. Finally, employees and customers should be able to harness the power of data to be able to achieve tangible results for the business.

For example, a factory manager can look up all these statistics of plant operations in a mobile dashboard to realize the ongoing targets, KPI's achieved as part of the operational technology. The Industry 4.0 does not stop at Information technology. It's a combination of operational technology combined with the powers of machines interacting with each other. The tools, accelerators, and methods provide required support to transform shop-floor into the state-of-the-art Digital factories with enhanced capabilities. This is the journey of Digital Business transformation – Industry 4.0. Let us start with the Industrial revolutions such as Industry 1.0, Industry 2.0, Industry 3.0 and finally the Industry 4.0 revolution.

Perhaps, you may know the first Industry revolution was primarily mechanical as Industry 1.0 a century ago. It scaled up-to large-scale production houses as Industry 2.0 post invention of electricity and mass scale usage in an early 19th century. Eventually, these initiatives transformed all the way to Industry 3.0 revolution, which is basically computers and the Industrial Internet revolution of the 20th century. Finally, it evolved into the fourth generation known as the Industry 4.0 revolution in the 21st century. You're witnessing these changes happening right now across the globe with AI, Big data, IoT, AR, VR and mechatronics with the enhanced network to allow machines communicating with each other. In smart robotics, it has further extended into cognitive intelligence to be able to make quick decisions, which can adapt depending on the requirements.

In the last decade, Industry 4.0 revolution started in Germany and expanded to other parts of the globe. On one hand, technology is evolving to the next generation platform known as the 3rd generation Technology platform, to make applications user-friendly with advanced in-memory capabilities to be able to process data real-time. For example, SAP has released SAP S/4HANA and C/4HANA, which are the largest investments by the software provider in the last 4-5 decades.

The objective is to leverage capabilities of in-memory computing by using required hardware (H/W) capabilities with large random-access memory (RAM) to store data in-memory to read data in real-time for analytics processing known as OLAP. Thus, database applications evolved from transactional processing systems (OLTP) to analytical processing systems (OLAP).

Furthermore, SAP is investing into the next generation digital technology framework known as 'SAP LEONARDO', which is the platform that integrates core technologies such as robotics, AI, AR, Visualization, mobility, cloud etc. This is the power of computing combined with machine learning that can help robots to think and act as autonomous machines. Every day Google is adding over a hundred services developed using machine learning programming that gets smarter day-to-day with advanced AI capabilities. Eventually, each of these devices will turn autonomous. A similar transformation is going on in Microsoft (AZURE), Oracle (OCS) and Cisco.

This book is designed to help you understand the Digital Transformation strategies to evolve into the next generation computing by integrating all departments within your organization to work as one Digital unit focusing on the transformation. Also, this book focuses on understanding the Digital Transformation basics and where to start from and how to enable the transformation. It helps you to de-mystify what is the real Digital transformation and what is not.

As you read this book, you will learn the evolution of Digital Transformation strategies, which is the next wave of a transformation of the I.T landscape. This includes databases, application systems with architecture supporting the business requirements. However, this transformational journey is not just limited to the information technology (IT) changes. It will drive change to the business process across various departments in changing revenue models with a simplified process. This change will provide deeper insights into technology as a next generation platform supporting business requirements, to plan the transformation to Digital journey. Hence, organizations must prepare themselves for disruption and none can be static in today's growing market.

The concept of 'smart' phones, smart homes, smart refrigerator, and smart factories is getting more and more common, as it indicates AI capabilities. It's becoming part of your day-to-day life. You must comprehend that the Digital age is disruptive; however, the benefits are immense in terms of increasing the value proposition to the customers, partners, employees and all stakeholders involved. Hence, companies have started embarking on the journey of Digital Transformation. Let us embark on the ambitious Digital Transformation journey!!!

The Digital Transformation - Industry 4.0 will help you to understand transformation strategies and implementation methodology from an end-to-end perspective, to help you manage Industry 4.0 - Digital Transformation projects with successful case studies. Each topic discussed in this book will explain the background info regarding the transformation strategies with specific case studies to help you drive changes within an organization as a transformation leader.

This book is directed at corporate executives, IT Program Managers, Project Managers, and Business Leaders, Data Scientists, Freelancers and Consultants to understand the value proposition and operating model to evolve into Digital Transformation age, but is also a valuable tool for the IT/IS department to make decisions with deeper knowledge and understanding of the product. The Digital transformation is not just the technology change; it is indeed the strategy to drive operational model using technology as the backbone.

Wishing you good Luck & Success in the Digital transformation endeavor!!!

■　　■　　■

Chapter 1: Digital Transformation – Industry 4.0 Overview

The objectives of this chapter are to help you understand Industry 4.0 - Digital Transformation strategies to prepare and transform the organization into the global trend. In this chapter, we will explore the technology platform, usage of cognitive computing in the destination Industry 4.0 digital transformation. If you ask a question, who is the boss of the company...Most of you would say it is a customer. Of course, customer, who is enthralled with the products and services that are offered. A customer, who often buys products and services throughout the ordeal, is the boss. Now, imagine all these innovations, strategies are primarily to help organizations to win more business in the competitive landscape, and increase the bottom-line profit. The destination Industry 4.0 will help you build products with an enhanced user experience and a higher degree of employee and partner satisfaction.

Now, let's understand how to make customers happy? Perhaps, you need to re-work on strategy, develop new competencies, build new products, become agile, people-oriented, innovative, customer-centric, streamlined, and efficient and can leverage opportunities to change the status quo and tap into new information and service-driven revenues with Industry 4.0

With the advent of big data and analytics combined with artificial intelligence (AI) capabilities, it is possible to analyze marketing data from varied social media platforms. For example, sales and marketing data from Google, Amazon, Facebook, LinkedIn, Pinterest, and blogs can help you build meaningful analytic capabilities for

17

enhancing customer's services by harnessing multi-platform channels.

The technologies like IIOT, Real-Time Analytics, and Big-Data provides the ability to process large volume & variety of Data and makes it possible to analyze production data to identify frequent issues faced by the Industrial Units. The above analysis would help organizations to monitor and solve issues proactively and enables the Organization to build insights that can potentially help in building a long-lasting customer relationship. This can be a simplification of internal IT operations or automation of the plant or any business operations.

It is a wonder to see the shop-floors changing to the state-of-art facilities with robotics, drones, nanotechnology and Artificial Intelligence (AI) with automated processes to achieve perfection? Each of these tools would yield details about newer opportunities that exist. Furthermore, capabilities of devices talking to each other with the Internet of Things (IoT), network connectivity and artificial intelligence (AI/AR-reality) have improved productivity. The I.T. application landscape has changed to decision making analytic engines by combining the power of in-memory platforms for quicker data access. Thus, I.T landscape has transformed the shop floor environment to high technology oriented robotics to develop finished goods of higher quality without defects. The invasion of GPS technology has further transformed into driverless cars, trains, and airplanes.

Our human endeavor is reaching far beyond the planet to the distant moon, mars, and stars far beyond in the Universe. In another couple of decades down the road, a space rocket with an autopilot programmed to arrive in moon and Mars may take you around the universe as a world tour or submarines taking you deeper under the ocean. It's apparent that driverless cars are becoming a reality with geo-spatial technologies. In the future, number of accidents can be reduced with sensors combined with satellite-based traffic light control systems. These changes are happening right now. The retail industry is transforming from traditional brick and mortar organizations to the hi-tech industry. The shift in mindset is driving business with innovations from brick & mortar to state-of-art technology used as a backbone to drive continuous improvements in order to drive value to the busienss.

The business landscape is rapidly changing its approach from large retail stores to a combination of brick & mortar plus the e-commerce stores, mobile, business-to-consumers (B2C), business-to-business (B2B) sales channels spanning across geographies with multi-currency and marketplace options. There are legends such as Amazon, who has completely transformed e-commerce with the marketplace concept. Truly speaking, digital transformation is driving business to think globally and standardize their business process.

Thus, by leveraging technology, it has combined with drone-based delivery and logistics platform to support faster delivery of goods based on GPS mapping the nearest stores delivering the packages. Hence, it is obvious to re-structure organizations to adapt to the global changes by transforming to digital.

Fundamentally, you're connected like a media more than ever in this Digital Age. Therefore, we have enormous potential to do with technology. There is a constant conditioned mind with the dominant industrialized mindset. These traditional organizations that are averse to changes will need strong transformation leadership to propel to the wave of digital transformation goals. These innovations are only possible with an open mindset and a cultural transformation of innovativeness. Hence, there is a fundamental shift in the strategy is required at all layers of the Organization.

There are key questions such as:
- What are we here for?
- Why are we doing this?

- How will it make it better for the people around us?

It is important to understand agile business thinking known as design thinking with the sense of purpose. These questions will shift the gears from just doing it to the next level of doing it to perfection.

The Digital Transformation is a combination of strategy, application with an innovative approach using technology levers. The approach will need to be connecting and teaching each other with a willingness for the I.T and business teams to try out things differently and not risk-averse. There is enormous potential in each of you and collectively you can win many more miles to go towards the Digital Age of transformation. It is shifting to empower across societies with present and future mindset. It is a profound transformation of business and organizational activity, processes, competencies, and model to impact the society positively with the tangible outcomes.

The Digital Transformation is a journey to connect intermediary goals striving towards continuous improvements of processes, divisions and business ecosystems. The ease of doing business is more than ever with the consumable services from the service providers. With the cloud-based software services, it is easy to start up your business with the plug-and-play office with readily available infrastructure as a service (IaaS) that can be procured for the business in a couple of days. Indeed, you'd pay only for the usage of services procured based on the services consumption model. This is a significant achievement in the Industry revolutionizing into the Digital World.

Furthermore, with the advent of robotics, AI, things have changed in the shop-floor. The image of the rugged shop-floor has transformed into highly sophisticated robotics infrastructure. Indeed, there is no wonder in seeing robots in action in the heavy metal industries helping human brains to churn out more productivity.

The Digital Transformation will be effective from top to bottom of the Organization and its culture as the mindset of employees will change. In the center of the spectrum will be customer satisfaction using technology as an enabler to support innovation and growth. It's a strategy, process changes to optimizing the business process for enhanced customer satisfaction. It is a motive to do it better with a continuous improvement strategy from 'BAU' culture to bimodal architecture with the existing legacy landscape with an additional layer of digital technologies, thus enabling the shift to a digital mindset. This change will be done by the leadership to encourage new training, skills developments in the areas of machine learning, Artificial intelligence, IoT where devices can talk to the systems interconnected and big data analytics to support predictive analysis etc.

These are all not just tools to infuse technology into the organization; it will transform the traditional mindset to understanding the customer problems and doing more to stay ahead of the competitive curve, nearest to perfection. In this evolutionary process, change is imminent with strong leadership to define a new strategy, innovation and a new culture with necessary organizational changes.

Thus, digital transformation is an art of deploying technology combined with organizational changes. There is no better time to start than to start right away to survive into the evolution of the future. Many organizations are embracing a new mindset of continuous, centralized, integrated change as part of the digital transformation.

The following four traits of Digital transformation leaders are essential to succeed in the endeavor:

1. Enabling constant change with the centralized and cross-organizational approach. Treating the customer as the boss with customer-focused

21

functions, which takes precedence and their efforts to common business practices

2. Talent retention and support in training and removing non-performing process roadblocks.

3. Investing in technology using a bimodal architecture that lets them run legacy systems effectively, while rapidly integrating new technologies.

4. In my view, these changes will integrate people, process, and technologies across the globe. Thus, it is evolving into a scalable platform, technology to adapt to the global trends and markets. The business model and the consumer behavior will change, thus setting the standards for the next generation.

Each of the above technology will take quanta of human intelligence to develop cognitive capabilities in machines to think and interact appropriately. With the enhanced machine learning, Google can operate devices, mobile platform and enable high-end data analytics with predictive capabilities with self-enabled grocery stores delivering products based on your need every month.

As you know, banking services from the traditional banking to the mobile banking has already become a reality. You'd no longer wait in the queue for the teller verifying cheque that you wanted to deposit. It's all in one-click of m-banking services in mobile, which would enable you to do it a lot faster and efficient with no paperwork. The stock market investments in NASDAQ is getting intelligent with predictive analytics venturing into investment technology, thus helping in finalizing the best stock pick of the day! It will help in reducing risks to the customers.

The enterprise mobile applications can do far more with a simple mobile that can turn into an enterprise in the hands of future humans. It can run enterprise applications, connect with devices for instructions in the factory model with seamlessly connecting the shop floor with a network of suppliers and distributors. It will help you with new product innovation, sales, and marketing, production, sales, and services. Thus, digital transformation is an outcome-based approach to analyze deeper, with a higher level of granularity with predictive analysis and data modeling to penetrate deeper into customer behavior. Perhaps, you'll be able to manage sales and marketing, manage sales orders, enjoying the sunset at the beachside by leveraging digital enterprise applications with high flexibility and reduced cycle time.

These are examples of digital transformation helping your business. On the other side of the simplification strategy, you can invest in the digital transformation of I.T operations to reap up enormous benefits. For example, repetitive ticket based application support services can be enhanced with the highest degree of automation to prevent major incidents combined with optimized human intellectual capital.

Thus, a combination of devices, platforms, strategy and innovative mindset with organizational change management and leadership will take you to the newer generation to scale-up operations. As an example, the entertainment industry has already changed from traditional movie theatres to the Netflix kind of on-demand sources to watch movies on-demand. The revolutionary skype and WhatsApp have transformed the telecommunications, whilst Hyperloop trains will change the commute forever. A similar invasion of digitization has broken the myths of large grocery stores into electronic sales via amazon.com as a platform with the capacity to include distributors and customers in the technology platform to choose the best products of their choice. Further, each of the customer behaviors is analyzed and the system analyses the customer behavior and helps them to make quick decisions. This is based on big data/analytics and AI platform. Each of these business practices has fundamentally shifted the mindset of individuals in the industry. You're not left behind as a consumer. The revolution in the industry is happening here and now.

You've constantly updated yourself about the upcoming changes in app stores to the Amazon store and the festive seasons flooded with favorite brands available at half price. There is always some kind of data analysis going on in the background based on customer interface with e-commerce sites. For example, Amazon.com reads customer sales patterns, to suggest products that a customer might be interested based on user preferences. Therefore, the world is striving towards near perfection with the technology enablers to predict the market, to support sales and distribution of the products. Thus, the new age tools would enable customers to focus on the business strategy, whilst the platforms will transform the Information technology (IT) to operational technology (OT). Perhaps, some of you know the time-consuming efforts of generating sales data from the hierarchical database systems (DB). Furthermore, in the process of simplification, reports were generated easily in windows based platforms which are easy to run, generate a report for the key user, as windows provided an enhanced user experience (UX).

In fact, you'll be amazed by the transformation of products suite in the enterprise products. For example, SAP R/2 transformed over a period into SAP R/3, SAP Enterprise Core Component (ECC). Now, it has finally evolved to SAP S/4HANA and C/4HANA with SAP Leonardo framework for the Digital enterprise. A similar transformation is happening to the Oracle cloud platform (OCP) suite, IBM Watson, Infosys Nia, Accenture Innovation Lab to Microsoft Azure, which is scaling up-to support the digital enterprise. Similarly, Google is building its services for the next wave of technology. Microsoft Azure provides an application to enable your organization to transform based on the cloud platform. In my view, organizations cannot survive without embarking on this journey of Digital Transformation. This is the next wave of Industrial evolution known as the Industry 4.0 revolution, and the organizations will adapt to the digital framework to survive.

The Digital Transformation is the goal that every software service provider and product companies strive to achieve. For example, Amazon, Google, Microsoft, and Oracle are trying to excel in providing simplification and a better experience for the end-users with their innovative products. Now, let us explore the real meaning of Digital transformation, and what is in store for a corporate executive. How do you take up this ambition and strategic journey to the next level of leading the transformation by leveraging technology?

Did you know that Google has embarked on an ambitious journey towards Digital Transformation and a pioneer in Innovative products and services? There are over thousands of AI-based services for the Industry developed in the open source for customers. Perhaps, customers have the choice to procure these AI-services and customize it for the specific requirements. In my view, the traditional ERP model will transform into the next wave of Digital ERP Services based model. For example, every business process will be decentralized with a package of AI services to build a robust end to end business process scenario data model. I am sure; Google will challenge the traditional data stores to build its cloud-based data stores defying the relational concept itself.

In the end, data from disparate sources will need to be captured, harnessed and provide abilities to the Industries with AI capabilities by developing algorithms for AI using programmings such as Python, C+, C# or Java. These AI capabilities will completely make operations autonomous as smart Industries. The capability to think and make decisions will be the core algorithm in machine learning aiding the AI technologies. Every machine in the organization will communicate with one another using sensor-enabled devices. Hence, a huge storehouse of data is required beyond just the databases stored in the cloud infrastructure. This will transform database models, storage and retrieval with more and more real-time data available to make quick decisions and the decisions will be made by the autonomous smart machines and not by a human soon!

What is Digital Transformation?

The Digital transformation is a journey of optimizing people, processes, and technology with multiple connected intermediary goals. In the end, a goal is to achieve the highest possible operational excellence through continuous optimization across business functions. The enablers are Information Technology (I.T) / Operational Technology (O.T) ecosystem of an inter-connected age, where building the function of the right bridge of that journey to succeed in the transformation endeavor.

The term fourth Industrial 4.0 revolution has just begun with the advent of IoT, AI/AR, VR, big data & analytics, cloud computing, cyber-physical systems, robots and robots, chat-bots and edge computing joining the bandwagon of technology. These are the essential components of the fourth Industrial revolution. The digital transformation adoption rate has already picked up in the manufacturing sector with the larger role for the Industrial IoT with a strategic view and approach. Now let us explore more on the Industry 4.0 - Digital Transformation.

The goal of the digital transformation strategy is to create enhanced capabilities by leveraging the possibilities and opportunities of emerging technologies and result oriented, better and in more innovativeness. A digital transformation journey needs a staged approach with a clear roadmap and vision from the key stakeholders, by analyzing the limitations of an internal/external landscape. This roadmap will consider the end goals to set it up as the digital transformation de facto standards in the ongoing journey, as is change and digital innovation.

In summary, the Digital transformation refers to the transformation of business and organizational activities. It involves improving business processes, competencies and models by leveraging digital technologies in a strategic and prioritized way. This change will need a cultural change of traditional mindset, which is focussed towards innovation. Now, let us explore the various facets of Industry 4.0 - Digital Transformation and its evolution from Industry 1.0 to Industry 4.0, which are the de-facto standards in today's manufacturing.

Industry 4.0 - Digital Transformation

As human consciousness evolved from the stone-age, iron-age, fire-age, atomic-age to the internet and computer age, the corollary industries evolved in parallel from the first industrial revolution to the fourth industrial revolution. It is the survival of the fittest as we say which holds good for the Industries in the competitive landscape to achieve better productivity and cost-effective products to the market in less lead time.

The Industry 4.0 with its core Digital Components are illustrated below in Figure 1-1 is a transformation of manufacturing and other sectors into connected and digital manufacturing. It provides additional benefits, with a range of technological evolutions and possibilities to move beyond the sheer operation dimension towards the so-called fourth industrial revolution. In simple terms, Industry 4.0 represents smart factories with high-end platforms supporting plant operations with the ability to think and interact with each other seamlessly as one-unit. It's like a robot talking to the operations for purchasing, inventory and warehouse departments further evolving into next-generation autonomous machines with human intelligence.

Figure 1-1 illustrates the core digital components of Industry 4.0 below:

Industry 4.0

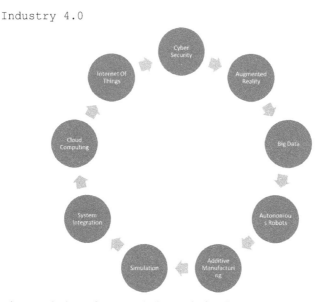

Figure 1-1 Industry 4.0 - Digital Transformation

The Industry 4.0 is the digital transformation started with manufacturing sector, leveraging the 3rd platform technologies, such as Big Data/Analytics and innovation accelerators, such as the (Industrial) Internet of Things, which refers to the communication between on-field devices to the operational technology such as sensors in cars that passes information about the maintenance of vehicle to the central system; and requiring the convergence of IT (Information Technology) and OT (Operational Technology), robotics, data and manufacturing processes to realize connected factories, smart decentralized manufacturing, self-optimizing systems and the digital supply chain in the information-driven cyber-physical environment of the fourth industrial revolution.

Though initial goals in Industry 4.0 were primarily automation, process improvement, and optimization; today, the benchmark standards are set up to the standards of innovation with newer business models with additional sources of revenue with information and services as cornerstones. The Industry 4.0 is also called 'smart industry' or 'smart manufacturing'. In many senses, it is related to the Industrial Internet. Thus, the evolution of Industry 4.0 standards has set the benchmark to revolutionize the Industry with the backbone of 3rd platform technology and devices with increased capabilities for predictive analytics and big data. The emergences of Digital transformation - Industry 4.0 has transformed the manufacturing, pharmaceutical, healthcare in every sector to improve smart capabilities by leveraging technology.

How do you achieve smart factory Industry 4.0?

The technology platform is known as the technology 3rd platform and key accelerators used for innovative products in the Digital Transformation (DX) economy, considering Information Technology (IT) and Operational Technology (OT) are the key parameters in the Industry 4.0. Further, Industry 4.0 is the information-intensive transformation of manufacturing in a connected environment of data, people, processes, services, systems and production assets with the generation, leverage and utilization of actionable information as a way and means to realize the smart factory and new manufacturing ecosystems. Now, let us analyze the evolution of the Industry 4.0 since the inception of Industry 1.0.

Industry 4.0 and the fourth industrial revolution

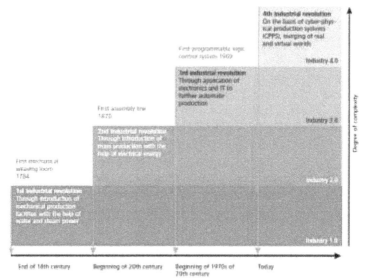

Figure.1-2. Fourth Industrial Revolution

As human intelligence evolved, the quest for innovation changed from just automating processes to transforming it to autonomous machines in the last few decades. Thus, the Industrial Revolution of steam engines moved to the advent of computers, internet and further into the world of mobility. Today, the world is moving towards enhancing capabilities to make machines smarter, with the human intelligence fed into it. Robotics used in the Industry can take appropriate actions to avert disaster and make intelligent decisions. The entire Industry is moving from just automation to the smart factories.

Now, let us analyze the four stages of the Industrial revolution as illustrated in Figure. 1-3 below:

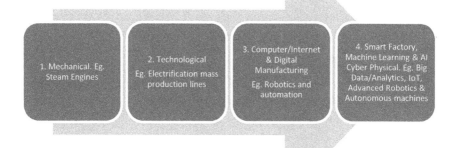

Figure 1-3 Industrial revolution

1. The first industrial revolution started with the introduction of mechanical production facilities such as steam machines, the usage of water and steam power. For example; Inventions such as trains, manufacturing units.

2. The second industrial revolution is where electricity and new manufacturing models arrived such as the assembly line production, which led to mass scale production with industrial automation.

3. The third industrial revolution introduced higher networks such as LAN, WAN and electronics and IT with increased robotics usage in manufacturing and connectivity with the arrival of the Internet.

4. In the fourth industrial revolution, innovative mindset got deeper with the usage of cyber-

physical production systems (CPPS), mobility and transition from just the internet.

Thus, paving way for the Digital and physical environments. On one side, technology has evolved with the increased capabilities of AI, robotics for machine operations etc. On the other side, the capabilities of data mining and predictive analytics improved. Thus, a combination of data, process, and machine operational optimizations lead to a 3rd technology platform which comprises of man, machines, process and automation with tools to build next-generation smart industries that are completely autonomous with the ability to think and act.

The convergence of Information Technology (IT) and Operational Technology (OT), with technologies such as IoT, big data, cloud with additional accelerators such as advanced robotics and AI/cognitive which enable Industry 4.0 with automation and optimization into next generation innovative manufacturing.

Therefore, the advent of AI, hyper-connectedness and data analysis into how things, machines, communicate, act and lead to insights with the Internet of Things in virtually every piece/machine of the Industry 4.0.

Now, let us explore the core digital components of Industry 4.0 as illustrated below in Figure 1-3 below:

Figure 1-4. Convergence & Application of Industrial Technology
--

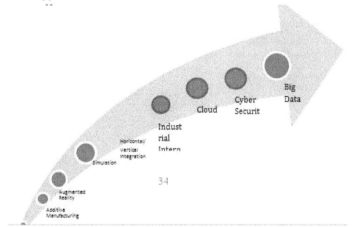

Figure 1-4. Convergence

As illustrated above in Figure 1-3, Industry 4.0 refers to the convergence and application of core digital industrial components listed below:

1. Smart Robotics,
2. Smart manufacturing (3D Printing),
3. Cognitive systems (Augmented reality, AI/VR)
4. Virtual Simulation,
5. Horizontal/vertical integration,
6. Industrial Internet of Things (IIoT),
7. The cloud,
8. Cybersecurity and
9. Big Data and Analytics.

It's clear that today some companies have invested in a few of these technologies; predominantly the traditional pillars of the 3rd platform such as cloud, Big Data / Analytics and, increasingly in the Industrial Internet of Things (IoT) from an integrated perspective. Let's explore core technologies that help in digital transformation as part of the 3rd platform as illustrated in the Figure 1-4 digital transformation accelerators.

1. Big Data / Analytics

The Big data/analytics computing plays a pivotal role in transforming organizations to digital. Every day organizations generate massive amounts of data; however, the challenge is to build capabilities to harness data to make meaning business insights. Today, with the increased network bandwidth capacity, handling loads using in-memory platform for real-time analysis using SAP S/4HANA or any other DB platform is not a big problem. However, the challenges are in transforming data into meaningful insights for the business. Big Data is the core technological bridge between the information management and computing technologies of the 20th century and those of the 21st century; it is also a bridge between the ways that organizations used to make critical day-to-day decisions. This is far more efficient data-driven decision-making that market leaders leverage today.

From financial forecasting and logistics to retail design and advertising, Big Data is the foundation upon which smart businesses build their operations. It's important for organizations to invest in harnessing big data by including cloud-based eco-systems involving hybrid integration between on-premises and clouds systems for flexibility.

2. Cloud Computing

The Cloud computing provides provide unlimited and scalable access to every function once performed by traditional I.T. systems from data storage and computing capacity management and use of software solutions.

Key advantages of Cloud:
- Low upfront infra investments
- Easy to implement and customize with a subscription-based model
- Reduced license, maintenance and staffing costs

The shift from the CAPEX-focussed model to OPEX model
Flexibility in infra resources ramp-up

A simple analogy of Artificial Intelligence is the capability to think and react to the environment. Now, let us understand the basis of machine learning, which aids in AI technology. Let me ask you a fundamental question before we start learning AI concepts:

What is thinking?
Well, you'd say, I believe it is my mind/brain etc.

Of course, true, But, how do you think?
You'd essentially think about the instances, environment that provoked the situation based on past experiences, present circumstances with the result in the future. Finally, you'd respond back to the environment in the current situation, isn't so?

It's your ability to react to the environment needs based on the experience, present circumstances. This is exactly what ancient Indian mystics identified as 'Thirikal Naan' which means the knowledge of an experienced person, who will not just react, instead evaluate the past instances with the current situation to predict future results. Now, you're AI machines are turning into mystics that can help you at the office to home.

Okay. Now, coming back to the point of human ability to think and process information. Can I state that human consciousness has evolved with the ability to store data in mind and brain and then help him retrieve information in the current situation to act...It is a wonder that Nature has provided the super bio-computer called mind to record data

35

in precision with hardware called a brain. This simple analogy is good enough to explain the concept of Artificial Intelligence (AI).

Now, imagine you've created a robot and programmed it using machine learning-AI technology by developing the basic algorithm. As you feed in data over a period, say after a few years, your robot will develop capabilities for processing information based on the data already available in the system. This algorithm can be done using machine learning.

Today, availability of data across Industries is not a problem; we have data worth 100+ years of history. However, the real challenge is to identify ways to harness it for making intelligent decisions. If you're enabling AI-technology, then naturally each of the Industries will become autonomous as you feed years of data. Obviously, it will become smarter than human. Then, there can be challenges between man and the machine. Let's not be alarmed by machines taking over as portrayed in the Terminator movie. However, the fact of the matter is that in every decision making in the future, there will be intervention from the machines. Then the challenge between man and the machine will exist. Luckily, human beings are endowed with emotions, which can never be realized by machines. The emotional quotient of human consciousness and brain functions combined with a bio-magnetic mind can never be replicated by machines as Nature's algorithm is far more sophisticated.

The bio-magnetic circuit with billions of neurons in the human brain is very sophisticated, and doctors will comprehend that the human brain cannot be replicated by machines in totality. So be proud of yourself for what you're right now, regardless of the color, creed, nationality etc. by the grace of the Divine Nature that you're ALIVE. Every cell in your body is carrying so many things that you can't even imagine. You've billions of neurons processing information every second. You're so privileged to use the human system without even thanking Nature for the wonder. But the fact is that machines can aid you in solving the most complex problems and decision making in every field. It will positively impact the society.

3. Cognitive Computing

The Cognitive computing also referred to as artificial intelligence (AI) is not new. The AI arrived decades ago in training military and space research and development. Perhaps, it was expensive and not scalable for enterprise applications. What is interesting in AI is the fact that systems gain capabilities to think. This is based on the systems that combine the power of machine learning, real-time data analysis and pattern recognition that is like the human thought process. Thus, the idea behind AI is not to program computers; it is to build the capabilities to think to become autonomous based on data consolidated, processed and utilized using specific algorithms to make intelligent decisions. The first step towards thinking process is data collection and then process and analyze using specific algorithms as illustrated below in Figure 1-4:

Figure 1-4 Cognitive computing

Furthermore, AI uses simple, intuitive, natural language interfaces. Cloud helps in storing massive data required for analysis. Thus, human-like thinking can instead be built into the Cloud. For example, IBM, Watson AI is one of the robust platforms for various industries, from healthcare and medical research to crime-fighting and marketing. Google with its vast ecosystem of libraries and languages, and Microsoft, with its flag firmly planted at the Centre of the Cloud API Azure world. The current state of Cognitive Computing offers two distinct opportunities for the technology. The first involves AI aided human tasks, in which intelligent computers assist humans in making decisions and performing tasks. The second involves intelligent automation, which eliminates the need for human involvement altogether. The current estimate is $150Billion USD by the end of 2020. We believe the AI game has started in every industry. As part of the Industry 4.0 – Digital transformation, AI plays a pivotal role in transforming industries to be autonomous. Let us explore each of these applications.

4. Mobility

In our view, the advent of mobile has completely disrupted the traditional ways of working. The enterprise mobility was a myth a decade ago, with the improved bandwidth and network connections, enterprises are depending on the mobile applications with the improved platforms and device capabilities increasing day-by-day. It's possible to do an analysis of employee self-service, manager self-service using apps and manage technology solutions using mobile apps. Therefore, enterprise mobile computing is a reality with increasing computing power to manage simple apps such as travel books to complex enterprise apps such as production process control, robotics, and drones and perform several other multi-tasks for a manager in one single mobile dashboard. Some of the keys AI applications to watch that fascinated me:

- Smart homes and smart offices
- Mobile AI assistant
- Self-driving vehicles
- Home health monitoring and diagnostic tools
- Service and companion robots
- Internet of Things (IoT)

IoT is a landscape of devices inter-connected embedded with electronics, software, and sensors that can collect and exchange data over a network. For example, common IoT devices are smart TV's, smart appliances from coffee machines to refrigerators, fitness trackers, self-driving cars, and thermostats.

There are many examples in consumer products such as a simple LED system that alerts with local weather forecasts to the pet's water bowl equipped with a sensor to alert the user to mobile, whenever water level goes down beyond critical point. These are known as enhanced objects that will turn into intelligent machines with the advent of IoT. Also, there are thousands of IoT devices used for industrial purposes ranging from smart-logistics, robotics to self-driving cars. I have heard a cardiac surgery done by robots in recent times. These applications will boost productivity; streamline logistics and lower operational expenses. Thus, it improves the utility of common tools and better connects organizations and teams to vital day-to-day data to make decisions.

IoT usage in Manufacturing
There is a massive potential in the usage of IoT devices in the Manufacturing sector, thus transforming into smart manufacturing units. It's no longer a shop-floor; it will be state-of-the-art technology factories using automation and robotics. Some of the key challenges in manufacturing are to reduce inventories, optimize supply chain and accelerate production and improve services. How do you achieve all of that?

This smart manufacturing is not just limited to production optimization; however, it helps -in safety and security. It can also be integrated into smart grids to optimize utility requirements. One of focus of the smart manufacturing is to improve maintenance optimization, and governance on intelligent maintenance Systems (IMS) to help monitor Industrial IoT. The Objective is to achieve near-zero breakdown of equipment using IoT-based analytics.

Infrastructure & Environmental Monitoring:

You might have heard about the smart cities. The concept is interesting to inter-connect cities to address main problems such as traffic regulation, energy demands, water, power, broadband utility demands, air/water pollution control, recycling etc. The objective of smart cities is to layer networks of sensor, device, and data to help cities optimize themselves, provide security much like smart grids but on a far more complex and layered scale.

Finally, smart cities will be able to be autonomous in managing energy demands and production, manage utility demands and traffic control etc. It can be extended to re-cycling, environmental pollution control to improve the quality of life in cities. Further usage of IoT can help in alert systems for tsunamis, earthquakes, and other disasters, and provide ubiquitous connectivity for residents and visitors.

6. **Virtualization**

Virtualization refers to the process by which the program or system creates a virtual version of something real or imaginary. You might have heard about the H/W virtualization, which refers to the connected computers to create the virtualized environment.

- **Virtual Reality** – This is a real breakthrough technology that helps customers to feel as if it was real. It helps in engineering product design and development. The VR device creates a virtual environment by replacing actual surroundings with a digital project of the 360-degree virtual environment. It started off with the entertainment, gaming industry and now the focus is on industrial virtualization technologies to help in training.

For example, VR is used extensively in military warfare techniques, air force which is hard to gain real-time experience of war. Furthermore, VR technologies have evolved in real estate to have the 360-degree view of the new house to buy or rentals etc. I was really amazed by a travel company showcasing the cruises. Of course, users can get a glimpse of it without having to leave the comfort of their home. Virtual reality allows to walk through a gallery, point of interest at any time, anywhere and its industrial usage is increasing day-by-day applications.

For example, collaborating with the business is the key to a successful project. Now, imagine global enterprises with multiple offices, each of their employees can effectively collaborating using VR, without a physical presence to the venue.

- **Augmented & Mixed Reality** – The AR technology is not virtualized or transformed. Usually, AR technology uses devices such as a screen to add virtual layers to the user's environment. Thus, the reality is augmented. Reality is thus augmented. For example, Augmented Reality is built in surfaces such as mirrors, helmet, windscreens and mobile devices. It allows a user to view details about an object or location to view on the screen.

For example, you'd have noticed landmark buildings in London that can be viewed with historical views of how it looked over one hundred years ago with detailed information.

Recently, We read an article about digital mirrors in retail fashion outlets, where customers can view the outfit and compare different views of outfits. Thus, AR/MR gives flexibility to the customer experience and helps in making decisions. There is an increased trend in retail sales due to the AR/MR capabilities in a few stores. In the future, digital schools, universities will embed digital AR/MR technology to enable an enhanced user experience in learning. In the classroom, students will have googled type of VR goggles to listen to the lecture by experiencing the environments such as space-related or even high-tech

41

engineering and medical colleges will have AR/MR capabilities to enhance industry experience for students.

Mixed Reality is a hybrid reality, in other words, it helps users to tweak the virtual images to interact with the surroundings. The MR uses a hybrid goggle that provides the 360-degree digital project with motion capture technology that translates user gestures into commands.

1. 3D Printing Technology

The 3D printing technology is an amazing technology, also known as additive manufacturing. It is used for rapid prototyping, proofs-of-concept and part-production technology that is agiler, low cost and portable than its predecessors. Typically, 3D printing technology synthesis of 3D objects using computer modeling. 3D printers are flexible, helps you to innovate product as design can be changed, thus it is used widely in healthcare, consumer goods, and manufacturing sectors. Industry 4.0 and the Industrial Internet

The fourth industrial revolution has transformed the entire industry to the next generation process with the arrival of tools, accelerators and methods defined on top of 3rd technology platform encompassing Artificial Intelligence (AI), Virtual Reality (VR), big data/analytics, thus exhausting the core benefits of technology in manufacturing processes. Now, let us analyze the key differences between Industry 3.0 vs. Industry 4.0 as listed below with the technology Wave(s) emergence, leading to the Innovative mindset as illustrated in Figure below:

The evolution of Industrial internet from Wave (I) to Wave (III) is illustrated below in Figure 1-5.

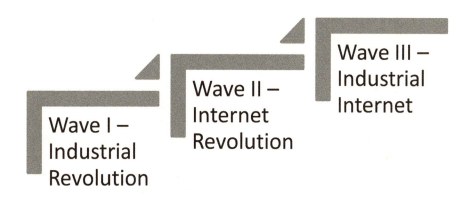

Figure 1-5. 3rd Industrial Revolution - The Industrial Internet.

Key considerations of the evolution of Wave (III) - Industrial Internet-Industry 4.0:

- Industry 4.0 emerged as the successful model with the power of computing, technologies with innovative mindset as illustrated above as Industrial Internet -Wave (III) is far superior to the Wave (I) and Wave (II).
- The Internet Revolution as illustrated above Wave (I) supported with enhanced computation power with the rise of distributed information networks.
- The Industrial Internet: This is called the fourth Industrial revolution in Industry 4.0. In the Industrial Internet view Industry, 4.0 is the 3rd Industrial innovation wave. Today the concept of 4th Industrial revolutions is the standard set by the Industry with the Industrial Internet Consortium. In the context of Industry 4.0 framework is known as RAMI 4.0, which standards for the Reference Architecture Model for Industry 4.0.

How are manufacturing companies doing?

Now, let us explore the adoption rate of the manufacturing companies to evolve into Industry 4.0 standards set by the Industrial Internet consortium. The roadmap for the Industry is clear, however, the stages to achieve this feat of success comes from the strong leadership, change management with a visionary leadership to transform shop-floors to the state-of-the-art facilities. Clearly, Industry 4.0, is the way forward in the digital transformation of manufacturing, however, most of the organizations are in the first state and has not realized the 'maturity' from a benefit and potential perspective. The primary objectives of the manufacturing industry are to transform to the smart factories by integrating information technology (IT) and operational technology (OT) systems to optimize operations.

Most of the manufacturing companies are not upgraded to the latest technologies, platforms and cutting-edge robotics. These companies continue to survive with an existing revenue model, current technology usage with very little spending on innovation. Hence, there is a strong leadership required to drive digital transformation as a top-down approach. This will mitigate risks. Some of the key benefits of Industry 4.0 standards include:

- Enhance productivity,
- Reduce costs by optimization of the operational processes
- Improve operations by using IoT to support the productivity of devices and Predictive maintenance as part of smart maintenance in services

Now, let us explore various stages of implementing Industry 4.0 - Digital Transformation.

Industry 4.0 in 2017: the first stages of maturity

You've heard about various maturity models and evolution of optimizing processes, resources to improve productivity etc. However, there is no robust method to transform the industry into the granular layer as every department worked in silos without an integrated top-down approach, thus lacking granularity in the approach. As a result, most of these organizations are not able to realize tangible benefits or ROI of technology spending. You must understand the digital transformation is not restricted to technology.

It encompasses everything from the way customers perceive products, innovation and employees adapt to design thinking, which is the outcome-based approach. The digital transformation will help you seize opportunities at all levels in the organization. In other words, the digital transformation will yield tangible benefits to all stakeholders if deployed correctly. Indeed, Industry 4.0 is the standard and the tsunami of transforming legacy to digital transformation. Obviously, this transformation will be disruptive, with strong leadership; you'll be able to mitigate the risks of failures. This is not the technology layer or the business process. It encompasses everything from the way users think, customers behave to the evolution of the product.

Most of the companies are implementing Industry 4.0 but in rather an ad-hoc basis and in isolated ways. This is the same phenomenon we see in any industry that is in digital transformation. It's that first stage in a broader ecosystem of possibilities as organizations move from obvious goals to true innovation and even disruption.

The Figure 1-6 illustration below shows some aspects of this broader ecosystem of possibilities, beyond the enhance productivity dimension.

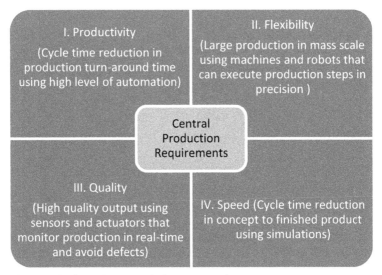

Figure 1-6 Industry 4.0 - Maturity

The enhanced productivity is just one part of the Industry 4.0, as you know most manufacturing and industrial companies are still are in that stage of planning. The Industry 4.0 ranks high on the agenda, yet in practice one or two isolated aspects of Industry 4.0 are implemented such as big data and robotics. This indicates the first stage of maturity whereby there is also a focus on the mentioned optimization and automation goals and gains, which is perfectly normal but it shouldn't stop there.

As the Figure 1-7 below shows, enhancing productivity, reducing costs and the automation of internal processes dominate. It's clear that in companies that are further from a benefits perspective and look at better customer service, new revenue streams, changes in business models and innovation, IoT deployments go further.

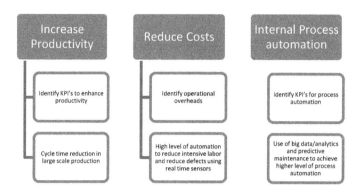

Figure 1-7. IoT in Organizations view

The internal goals and productivity improvement dominate most IoT deployments in the current maturity stage.

Summary

In this chapter, you've studied the evolution of Industry 4.0 – Digital Transformation and roadmap. Also, we discussed the high-level scope of transforming your Organization to the Digital World. Industry 4.0 – Digital Transformation will transform the organization to the next evolution of standards set by the Industry. These factories will no longer be plain shop-floors of mass productions. Instead, these factories will transform into revolutionary smart factories using AI/AR, VR, robotics, IoT, cloud, big data analytics to communicate to the Operational technology using 3rd technology platform stack & services with in-memory computing such as SAP S/4HANA. Thus, by combining the power of mobility, cyber-physical applications into developing next-generation smart factories to benefit customers.

In the end, these changes will help you to grow more productive, expand your market potential and reach out to the customers into emerging markets. You can harness data using autonomous decision-making engines or use AI capabilities in factories to build state-of-the-art facilities. Also, it leads me to believe that the next generation of technology will support clients worldwide by harnessing the power of innovative computing with a change in the mindset from just doing it to an innovative mindset. The breakthrough in the Industrial revolution from Industry 1.0 to Digital Transformation - Industry 4.0 has just begun with many more companies embracing the Industry 4.0 standards. This is a true Industry Revolution 4.0 – Digital Transformation!!! The journey has begun!

Now, let's look at the holistic approach on accomplishing this ambitious digital transformation journey in the next chapter.

■ ■ ■

Chapter 2: Digital Business Transformation – a Holistic Approach

The objective of this chapter is to delve deeper into the Digital Business Transformation with a holistic approach. This would help organizations to transform to the Industry 4.0 standards with a time-tested and proven framework discussed in this chapter. It is not implementing technology alone; indeed, it is the transformation of people's mindset; optimizing processes by leveraging technology in the Digital landscape with strong leadership. Now, let us explore the holistic approach in the digital business transformation journey.

In a broader context, Digital Transformation not only transforms business, technology, and disruption, it also implies changes to the society, government. It is imperative to decentralize shift of focus towards the edges of the enterprise ecosystem. As you know, the customer is at the center of the ecosystem with edges such as people, process, and technology. Now, let us understand the hyper-connectivity and focusing on the edges of the enterprise ecosystem as illustrated below in Figure 2-1 with core business areas, where you'll need to build your capabilities across to survive the wave of Digital Transformation – Industry 4.0. It's important to understand 'what' and 'how' questions before embarking on the digital transformation journey.

- The What: Using digital technology to transform
- The How: Envisioning your transformation journey and how to make it happen

For example, in large enterprises those are running for decades will go through significant challenges. In the manufacturing sector, typically people are focussed towards plant operations. In this context, the I.T operations scale up over a period and every department works as silos. In most of the large enterprises, I.T landscape is complex to manage. These applications evolved over a period with no common vision or integration. Thus, every department ends up working in silos. For example, the analytics team trying to support sales data will need to consolidate data from various legacy systems, finally spending hours in data extraction without being able to provide business insights. Eventually, integration became overly complex and a daunting task in every new project implementation, resulting in carrying large overheads. Though these companies had the vision to standardize approach for decades, it became mission impossible to bring people, process, and technology platform to the common ground.

Each of these I.T applications, supporting users with many complex interfaces, integration scenarios from the engineering application to the ERP application. The complexities scale increased over a period due to a large number of customizations and business requesting for more specifications. As a result, the cost of I.T landscape maintenance increased year-on-year. There were about ~ 200+ applications, some were working in silos. Hence, there was a compelling need to migrate some of the applications to replace with modern technologies.

Large digital transformation consulting companies have looked at various enterprises to classify them into:

- Beginners – People, who're not doing anything in digital
- Conservatives – People, who're driving transformation into the narrow area. For example, Asian paints invested in supply chain and then stopped.

- Toppers - Those who invest and take-up challenges immediately, however without proper governance.
- Digital Leaders - who really understand and implement a digital transformation program

Perhaps, you've realized that changing mindset of a factory worker or any user will be a challenge. Obviously, there was strong resistance to changes within the organization. Finally, the company challenged their own employees, organization structure with ways of working, conducted several training programs as part of the change management strategy. With continuous communication and improvement plans, finally, employees adapted to the newer trends and technologies. The above example is one aspect of the story. There are many companies where different stakeholders have their own views and difficult to adapt. For example, a migration from ORCL to SAP or vice versa is a difficult change. A fundamental shift in core technologies, ways of working and innovative mindset will be challenging tasks to accomplish. Most of the above-mentioned risks can be mitigated by strong leadership by providing roadmap, vision, mission, effective change management and engagement with the buyers, vendors, partners, employees, and customers. It's a challenging task for a leader to demonstrate his digital transformation vision. By setting up small journeys to perceive the results that would pay-off in the long-term.

Today, customer satisfaction is important to succeed in the business. For example, a customer can download music, expect the best of the music and pay online and consume services. Hence, it is imperative for companies to build foundational architecture by developing re-usable business services. For example, retinal scans for document signature. If your able to support such a change and integrated within the organization will help you succeed in the endeavor. The plan for digital transformation will encompass:

51

- Change management – training for digital knowledge
- Talent management – for digital skills &
- Mechanism – adapt to the customer needs such as key performance indicators (KPI's)

Now, let us understand the core business areas of focus to define the transformation goals and objectives. It is important to focus on the core functions as part of the journey to ensure successful digital transformation as illustrated below in Figure 2-1 core functions.

Digital transformation core functions

Figure 2-1 Building capabilities across Core Business areas

It is important to understand each of the above-illustrated core business areas to build your capabilities around. This is the first step in the Digital Business Transformation journey to strengthen the core components of the business. As a Digital leader, you should be cognizant of the disruption across various business units within the organization, however with effective change management and leadership; these risks can be mitigated with the right usage of people, process, and technology as enablers.

There are around 9 core business areas as listed below:

- Identify Core Business areas
- Focus in key Business Processes
- Improve critical Business models
- Improve business ecosystems
- Identify tools, accelerators, and methods as reusable technology assets
- Evaluate Organizational culture and change management
- Leverage Partner ecosystems &
- Improve ways of working (wow) with partners, customers and employees.

In most of the organizations that are spending a lot of money in I.T. Run operations to manage the BAU is getting overly complex day-by-day. On one hand, I.T landscape is increasing with custom applications; hence it is difficult to manage. On the other hand, customers are asking for more innovative services. Overall managing the IT landscape and infusing innovative changes to the applications is very challenging. The current need of the hour is to identify critical process areas and re-model the landscape as per the business requirements.

The IT landscape must be flexible, adaptive to changes as we progress. As business is re-shifting its focus with continuous improvements, IT should also support the innovation as a backbone of the business operations. For example, if a business decides to implement Internet-of-Things (IoT) and robotics technology in the factories, warehouses, then I.T should be scalable to adapt to the trend and support business to do more. Thus, tools, accelerators, and methods of technology should quickly regroup to support the business operations to make customers happy.

Let us explore each of the above components of transformation that are vital to any organization in the Digital Business Transformation journey. Though enhancing customer experiences is one of the primary goals, however, it is important to understand the impacts and risks across various components of the business as discussed below. Each of these parameters will need to carefully evaluate for a successful implementation of the Digital Business Transformation. You'll need to define KPI's in each of the above functions to ensure a transformation goal.

Identify Core Business Functions - These are the core functions such as human resources (HR), Production, Sales & Marketing, Supply Chain, Services and Operations and Customer relationships management that predominantly drives the business. It's important to identify improvements in the core business functions.

In one of the manufacturing organization, there were complex business processes in managing recruit to hire process. Most of these operations from the job posting to recruitment was all done manually. Finally, the company implemented SAP Success Factor to manage job postings, recruitment with approval workflow to reduce cycle time by >50%. A similar analogy in customer relationship building from prospect to customer phase; This strategy was implemented to enable relationship with the customer by implementing Sales Force, Finally, CRM-Sales Force helped to maintain a good relationship with the customer with increased sales. Thus, companies should identify top 3 core business functions that can be digitally transformed to improve the business process. This can be a combination of shifting the business model with enhanced technology support the transformation.

- **Focus on Key Business Processes** - As part of the Digital Transformation goals, it is important to focus on optimizing the business process. Your business operations, plant production order capabilities might need to improve based on key performance indicators (KPI's) in key business processes in the domains mentioned above in each function.

The key element of the business process transformation will help your organization to grow smarter and innovative. For example, P2P or O2C process involves life-cycle of procurement and sales processes. The various touch points in this cycle involve customers, suppliers, and employees. By digitally transforming the process aligned with the business goals, your critical business processes can be transformed.

Improve critical Business models – It's important to identify and improve critical business models. For example. There are ways to exhaust various sources of revenue streams in various platforms such as mobility, e-commerce channels of sales and marketing, websites and blogs to market your products and services with a go-to-market approach. Thus, you've to focus on evolving business models to increase revenue. Amazon.com is a classic example of creating a new business model with distributor network online and revenue sharing models with increased product lines using an e-commerce platform.

Today, Digital Marketing is one of the key areas of focus. Most of these businesses have adapted to the newer ways of working by enabling a robust digital marketing strategy. Each of the platforms such as social media, mobile, and analytics can help in marketing your products and services more effectively to the masses across the globe. This is the evolving trend in the industry. Finally, the business model will need to be flexible to adapt to the customer requirements. For example, a car company launched a mobile app to customize your requirements. You can get as specific as you want to make customers happy. For example, a newer business model is evolving with the arrival of chatbots to open-up additional communication channels for customers. The entire communication platform is changing with every conversation with the customer is captured, harnessed from social media channels to build valuable insights to the clients. Thus, it is important to evolve assess critical business model and make the necessary changes to adapt to the digital transformation.

Identify business ecosystems with partnership model –

A new model of collaborative approach to enabling newer avenues of revenue is required. A partner ecosystem is essential to enable integration within people, process, and technologies. Often, specialist skills are readily available within your partner ecosystem. Further, newer strategies can be derived with the business process analysts available in the partner ecosystem to drive the journey of Digital Business Transformation rather effectively with a time-bound approach to drive results.

As a client, you may not necessarily have all the required skills to launch a full-fledged digital transformational program. However, it is possible to succeed with the support of niche consulting companies, who can help you with the transformation journey. As you know, building skills take a lot of time; hence it is imperative to seek good skills available in the market via partner channels.

Identify tools, accelerators and methods as reusable technology assets such as AI-assets to readily deploy as services – As you're embarking on an ambitious journey of enhancing your customer experiences, it is important to build reusable technology assets to achieve tangible outcomes in every phase of the project. One part of the organization focus is to build re-usable technology assets by leveraging tools, accelerators, and methods to effectively embark on the journey. However, it is important to ensure these assets bring in value-add to the customers, by adding value in terms of user experience and employees by easing operational issues, who are real assets to the organization.

One of the core aspects of a transformation journey is to identify skills and available tools. Perhaps, you can procure the necessary software tools that can help you to fasten the progression path to digital transformation. For example, a simple common communication platform can help you integrate your organization's communication requirements. However, you must avoid silos and start implementing common platforms, technologies to enable robust governance within the organization.

Evaluate Organization culture and change management - It is imperative to understand the current Organization culture with strong change management practices functional to enable organization-wide changes to the business model and operations. While, you're embarking on a journey of large magnitude, thus impacting all departments, it is important to understand the culture and make appropriate leadership decisions and empower employees with required skill developments and training as part of the transformation project. A strong leadership with quick decision making is required to enable a large digital transformation program. Most of the pitfalls of the transformation programs have occurred due to lack of strong leadership coupled with lack of effective decision-making on-time.

Most of the organizations struggle to implement change management due to lack of strong leadership and proper governance. If you're unable to enable a strong cultural change from factory mindset to digital mindset, it will be a huge challenge. Hence, you must educate, empower employees, partners throughout the journey of transformation, to succeed.

Leverage Partner ecosystems - It is important to communicate the goals of the Digital business transformation across all departments including the partner ecosystem. We do look at some less business-related 'Digital Transformation' phenomena with anticipated disruptions as a risk to the business, however, mitigate via proper change management planning and execution. Ultimately, the focus is on the business, which means a holistic digital transformation view to bring positive changes towards enhancing customer experience, technological evolutions and innovation with a clear purpose are very crucial for the successful implementation of the Digital Business Transformation projects.

We discussed more on the above topic of leveraging partner ecosystems. With the niche skills, tools & technologies available from the partner, it is prudent to quickly assess the situation and procure as necessary. This will help you in the transformation journey. While a client can stay focused on the end-goal and the business process, rest of the technology platform related solution design and implementation can be done with the skilled resources and technologies procured from the partner.

Improve Organization ways of working (wow) with partners, customers and employees – It's important to understand the current ways of working within your organization, dealing with internal employees, partners and customers etc. People should be empowered to perform the roles with an innovative mindset and respect for commitments to promote a culture of openness and acceptance within the Organization. A cultural transformation is required to be focused on customer-centric, enhanced user experiences, newer workplace models and changing partner dynamics with required change management in every department. By using technology effectively as an enabler to adopt a robust change in the longer run.

The ways of working is an important topic related to the change management within the Organization. You must ensure the end of the day, IT/Business key users across various departments are completely aligned, to appreciate the digital transformation and the solutions. This may lead to chaos initially, which can be resolved via constant communication strategy and training.

Outcome-based journey

Because of mitigating all risks with the right focus and approach the primary outcomes of any large Digital Transformation program is to develop tangible outcomes across the organization such as:

1. Increased awareness,
2. Decision making &
3. Agile execution

It is important to re-emphasize on the end goals, customer experience with partners and stakeholders to discuss disruption in the edges, which are the core components of the business. Indeed, the role of the organization is to connect all departments by creating one common vision of the Digital Transformation journey to overcome internal silos to reach the common goal. These changes may address technology approach with a shift from traditional to value-add services based operational shift with the advent of cloud and SaaS-based offerings to ease supporting ongoing business operations. These changes in the technology, as well as the decentralized approach in business models and technology shift, can aid towards an aggressive pursuit in the journey of Digital transformation projects. For example, Technology has already been decentralized with the cloud, SaaS, IoT enabled decentralized cybersecurity. Now, let us analyse various disruptions caused by the Digital Business Transformation.

As we discussed 8 core aspects of digital transformation, each of you would agree the transformation journey is an uphill task with a lot of disruptions to the business. As a Digital champion, you're going to ask the business to change the ways of working and ask sales to identify additional revenue models. To say the truth, the digital transformation will cause a lot of disruption to the business, customers, partners, technology and employees in the respective domain areas.

Digital disruption

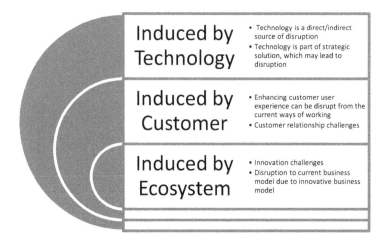

Figure 2-2 Digital Disruption

As discussed in the earlier chapter, Digital disruptions occur in the core business areas, we have identified nine core areas. These disruptions are driven primarily by the customer, technology, ecosystem and innovation as illustrated in Figure 2-2. These disruptions can be the result of changing customer behaviour and market context changing their strategy, innovative mindset leading to the newer business models, products and services etc. In the end, the goals of the digital disrupt are to enhance customer user experiences with new product lines and innovative service offerings. Primarily, disruptions as a human phenomenon are caused by changes in the way people use technologies with expected outcomes.

For example, businesses have evolved with the use of technology for changing the user experiences, such as mobility. With enhanced mobile apps, it is possible to give an enhanced experience to the customers with varied buying options. Thus, e-commerce sites have changed the consumer behaviour in the Industry. The Digital transformation in the BFSI sector is enormous, with the advent of m-wallet payments using the mobile app to make payments digitally. Furthermore, advent of Cloud, big data and analytics help in analysing customer behaviour more closely, whilst cloud can ease out the day-to-day operational overheads. These digital disruptions are positively impacting consumer behaviour.

Thus, the evolution of Artificial Intelligence (AI), Internet of Services (IoT), Virtual Reality (VR) combined with Cloud subscription-based offerings, big data and analytics have finally evolved as a 3rd Technology platform for the Digital Business Transformation. The tools, accelerators offered as part of IoT services are primarily used in the manufacturing and logistics sector for transformation. These are disruptive with the additive manufacturing and advanced robotics taking the centre stage positively to improve productivity in the evolution of Digital Business Transformation – Industry 4.0. Now, let us recap the three critical parameters that form the root causes of disrupt and transformation as illustrated above in Figure 2-2.

Root Causes of disruption and transformation

The four main factors causing digital disruptions are:
* Technology,
* Customer,
* Ecosystem &
* Innovation

Technology: Technology is a key enabler for any Digital Business Transformation projects; however, it cannot be the driver for disruption or transformation. It is how it is used by the customers, partners and stakeholders. The adoption rate of technology to transform business is essential; as a result, it impacts customers, partners and employees in a positive way in the ways of working (wow).

For example, a large enterprise running banking applications in legacy systems may be hesitant to change the ways of working. Now, imagine the transformation of technology to simply a mobile-based app. This may be easy to use and friendly for the customer, whereas the IT department should be skilled and scale up, and adapt to the challenges.

Customer: The customer demands are one of the primary drivers for the digital transformation. As you know, customer behaviour has changed and the demands are increasing in terms of products and services. Therefore, it is imperative for the business to take necessary steps to drive changes at the root levels of enhancing user experiences, simplifying tools, accelerators and methods to derive meaning responses to the customer in zero time.

Often, customers are the direct beneficiaries of the change. For example, a simple mobile app. Can help them change the design and request for custom specifications. With the flexibility and analytics, they can really integrate their design thinking into products.

The evolution of e-commerce, IoT's have changed the way customers look at products and services. It is no longer a static website that can offer products. It is how you help customers to customize products such as do-it-yourself and design, develop and order using mobile apps or even simple applications to envisage a product and design themselves. It's increasing with the enhanced user experiences and capabilities in mobile computing. Furthermore, big data and analytics yield tons of data about customer preferences and the buying options. These data points are harnessed by innovating new products and services. For example, a recent survey indicated customers have a choice to design their own variants of the high-end cars such as make-to-order specific scenarios are increasing.

Innovation: As we currently ride the wave of Industry 4.0 with the available technology tools, accelerators and methods, customers can have enhanced user experiences. In the end, innovative products and service offerings help organizations to invent rapidly with a continuous improvement strategy to stay ahead of the competitors. These innovations will have a profound impact on the society.

Most of the companies are not operating to the fullest potential due to lack of innovation. They may be used to a legacy application and not very flexible to enhance their skill, knowledge and scale-up to the innovative products and services. Hence, these large enterprises fail to meet constantly changing customer expectations. Today, the industry is envisaging an auto-plant, driverless car, auto-services and many more to replace repetitive tasks with an innovative solution. The AI machines can think and act, instead of reacting to a failure. This is a major breakthrough in the industry and this trend will continue to evolve in the future.

Ecosystem: The economic changes, demands from partners that you may want to adopt such as regulatory requirements of a specific geography etc.

Just imagine how all business processes are interlinked, from a customer perspective, the way information runs across all digital transformation. Hence, you'll need to build a solid roadmap with a vision to achieve the ambitious journey of transformation. You'll need to align with employees, partners and upcoming technology.

Speaking the same language

In a digital transformation journey, it is important to make sure all stakeholders are aligned. So, let us understand what initiatives are NOT parts of the Digital transformation journey:

- Digital marketing
- Digital customer behaviour

Implementing advanced technology doesn't mean digital transformation without tangible benefits. You should understand the Digital journey is different from just automating manual process such as paperwork.

Digital transformation – reality

As discussed in the earlier section, Digital transformation is not just about implementing advanced technology. For example, a large taxi company has changed the traditional business model of booking taxi, thus causing disruptive changes to the traditional way of bookings taxis using digital technologies to alter the existing models. You might have observed your travel app providing you preferences of travel. This is based on AI capabilities where the algorithm identifies your patterns. These patterns are analysed to make intelligent decisions to provide a final summary of upcoming travel planning. Based on the google search, cookies collect your preferences and store data transform and provide you short-cuts to the query for faster access. Google is no longer a search engine, it is a smart engine that can guide you through the navigation app or help you make decisions using the AI capabilities.

One of a large organization with over decades of raw data provided details to Google to harness it and make it useful for the forecasts. Google used this raw data by applying its algorithm to transform raw input data into useful analytics forecasts. It used machine learning capabilities to transform data into meaningful information. Further, this example can be applied to any Industry with raw sales inputs, customer behaviour of a pattern of factory issues can be transformed to meaningful analytics and more into AI to be able to predict and make decisions to avert decisions. The interesting part is not just about automating analytics and forecasts, instead, the AI capabilities are helping machines to make autonomous decisions based on the data consolidated so far. It's like human thinking before making decisions!

Indeed, this is a digital transformation by creating new markets and revenues. The above example of a large taxi company using the mobile app for booking taxi is a classic example of transformation. Its GPS enabled, you can estimate the exact time of arrival and departure to plan your activities. It's good to leverage technology to transform the business model, revenues, customer behaviour with improved security for the passengers etc.

End of the day, in the increasingly competitive landscape, only the taxi companies with enhanced mobility apps will survive in the market, as all another existing taxi model will vanish eventually. This is exactly what is happening in every Industry. Either you take the opportunity to Digital transformation of business models, enhance customer experience, in-house productivity by optimizing the process, resources and technology. Otherwise, there is no scope of your business to exist in a span of less than a decade from now. Let's have a closer look at the Digital transformation framework and its components. A digital transformation comprises of the customer at the centre stage with various business functions around the edges such as

- User Experiences
- Innovative products & services
- Sales & Marketing
- Optimized risks and
- Enhanced corporate controls

As illustrated in Figure 2-1 Digital Transformation Framework below. By leverage tools, methods and accelerators each of the above function is improved in the Digital world, thus by shifting the gears from the existing business model to the Digital business model and consumer behaviour.

Digital transformation framework

Figure 2-1 Digital Transformation Framework

The following table 2-1 highlights the transformation of the existing business model to Digital business model.

Customer	Operational	Business Model
Understanding the customer	Digitization of processes	As-is process modified to the Digital process
Top-Line Growth	Employee enablement	New Digital Business
Customer Touch points	Performance management	Digital globalization

Table 2-1 Digital transformation framework

The key areas of digital transformation include improvements to the core business areas:

- Enhanced digital customer experience with a mix of lean process improvements with cost savings.
- Innovative products and services with different business models
- Improve digital transformation in the core business functions such as Digital fulfilment, risk optimization with improved corporate controls.
- Digitization of sales and marketing and distribution to improve process efficiencies.
- Improved data analysis across by leveraging tools, accelerators effectively such as big data, analytics
- Improved customer relationship management (CRM) with tight integration with product support and contact centres real-time
- Improve ways of working with workforce engagement and collaboration across the organization with unified communication such as Skype, MS and social collaboration tools used for enterprise requirements etc.
- Improved learning and education solutions for continuous learning
- Finally, improvement in business functions such as procurement, supply chains and supplier relationships

It is important to perceive a visionary digital organization with all business functions, people and process interconnected and working seamlessly as one global unit with the technology used as an enabler.

Myths & Reality

Though Digital transformation is a key priority in many organizations, it is essential to understand the myths and reality. Often staged-approach with priorities defined will lead to any digital transformation projects. However, there are four key priorities that organizations should realize to impact key stakeholders as part of the journey.

- Managing the Business/IT relationship
- Realizing common DNA of transformation
- Lead by example, by starting your transformation journey right away as a leader &
- Transformation leads by the Top-down approach

Now, let's explore each of these parameters closely.

- Managing the Business/IT relationship:

It's important to maintain a good relationship between Business/IT to derive common vision and goals to achieve as part of the Digital business transformation journey.

- Realizing common DNA of transformation:

The vision of leaders is to build a common DNA to succeed in the path of the digital transformation.

- Lead by example:

Instead of waiting for others to succeed, leaders do start early and accomplish. There is no point in waiting for others to succeed. As a leader in the Industry, envisage a roadmap, analyse digital roadmap, vision and goals to achieve and lead by example.

- Top-Down approach:

Finally, you'll need to understand the Digital transformation is led from the top-down approach with all key stakeholders involved.

The following table 2-1 refers to the Digital Transformation Myths vs. RealityThe following table 2-1 refers to the Digital Transformation Myths vs. Reality

SNO	Myth	Reality
1	Digital transformation is only about customer experience	Real Opportunities exist in efficiency, productive & employee utilization
2	Digital transformation is only Technology change	Opportunities exist across functions
3	Digital transformation is bottom-up approach	It is top-down approach
4	Digital initiatives will lead to transformation without much focus on digital leadership	Digital initiatives will only succeed with a proper leadership and focus
5	Relationships between IT & Business does not really matter	It's key to succeed as Business and IT should be aligned with common goals
6	Digital transformation approach differs from one industry to the other	The fundamental DNA is same
7	We can wait to see the change happen	Leaders start the initiatives right away with clear vision and roadmap

Summary

In this chapter, you've studied the Digital Business Transformation approach. Just to recap, we discussed nine core business processes and functions to focus as part of the journey. The Digital transformation framework helps you focus on the priorities. We studied the myths and realities of transformation, without losing focus on the goals and objectives set by the Digital leaders. We talked about the digital disruptions across various departments and ecosystems to manage through strong change management practices adopted.

The Digital Business Transformation – Industry 4.0 is just not about setting a few digital initiatives and let go. It is the DNA of the organization with a fundamental shift in the ways of working with customers, partners and employees. It is not about enforcing a few technologies and automates processes; digital transformation is a well thought and laid plans to implement over stages to achieve tangible outcomes in every stage of the transformation journey. The starting point could be good organizational behaviour between the business/IT, thus enhancing relationships with employees, departments and partner ecosystems with an innovative mindset. This change will help employees to innovate and experiment without being risk averse.

In the next chapter, we will explore the Digital transformation strategy & roadmap.

■ ■ ■

Chapter 3: Digital Transformation – Strategy & Roadmap

The objective of this chapter is to delve deeper into the Digital Transformation strategy & Implementation with specific case studies of successful Digital Transformation journey across Industries. This chapter will help you to understand Industry 4.0 standards with a proven framework.

Further high-level discussions related to the Reference Architecture (RAMI) model, which would help you set priorities of the Organization in the transformation journey. As discussed, it is not a project to implement the technology. It is a transformation journey of people's mindset to optimize business processes. Now, let us explore the holistic approach in the digital business transformation journey.

What is the right strategy for transformation; this is the general question being put forward before a company embarks on the digital transformation journey. The digital Transformations is all about keeping in mind below outcomes across all industries as highlighted by Mr. Satya, NADELLA, Microsoft:

1. Empowering Employees,

2. Engaging Customers and consumption model,

3. Optimize operations and &

4. Transform products

How can these be achieved, the answer could be building solutions around

1 Modern workplace

2 New Product Innovations, Business Applications

3 Optimization by analyzing opportunities in the new business model, newer revenues, products & services

4 Data & AI (Transform Products and optimize operations using AI & Cognitive learning such as IBM Watson, SAP Leonardo, Google cloud platform etc...)

The ability to digitally reimagine the business is determined in large part by a clear digital strategy supported by leaders, who foster a culture, with the ability to change and invent the new. What is unique to digital transformation is that risk-taking is becoming a cultural norm as more digitally advanced companies seek new levels of competitive advantage. The employees across all groups want to work for businesses that are deeply committed to digital progress. Thus, digital leaders will need to keep this employee expectation in mind, to attract and retain the best talent pool.

The key technology enablers used in digital transformation projects are:

S- Social

M- Mobile

A- Analytics &

C- Cloud

As highlighted in the earlier section, it's important to point out that Industry 4.0 is the standard framework of digital transformation. However, most of these organizations are still in the early stages of preparations for Industry 4.0, in the process of launching the transformation programme. The core vision of Industry 4.0 is far more studied and documented than that of other evolutions.

The Industry 4.0 is a vision and an established framework with a documented strategic roadmap towards realizing the vision. Let's compare digital transformation and the role in it of the Industrial Internet of Thing, which along with evolutions in mechanics, engineering, and manufacturing, essentially are what Industry 4.0 is about.

The Industrial Internet of Things (IoT) refers to the adoption of Industry 4.0, which happened in the individual context of an organization. However, Industry 4.0, which is about more than automation in manufacturing, which is the vision of digital transformation in the end. Industry 4.0 is a framework with reference models, roadmaps and well-described components, which is unique. Therefore, implementing digital transformation - Industry 4.0 requires a staged approach whereby the initiatives in the earlies maturity stages and areas ultimately lead to the realization of an integrated vision and reality. Yet, as opposed to digital transformation this vision requires deeper analysis combined with a structured approach to succeed in the transformational program. In the next section, let's explore the transformation roadmap with a real-time case study.

Case study

For example, SalesForce.com, a major CRM product based company has transformed from a CRM company to an AI/framework by leveraging AI/IoT, Python programming, and machine learning. Salesforce has considered several datasets to build the value-based outcomes into analytical data using build model. It helps field officers, sales engineers to collaborate real-time from lead generation to closing a sale. It's an enhanced version of the analytics. Now, let's explore the transformation roadmap. Perhaps, you'll be able to conceive ideas for your own organization. If you observe, in the above example, salesforce transformed from a product based company to completely digital, because they had explored the possibilities of autonomous actions and insights derived from sales data. It is not just about how many sales you're making, more so into the nitty-gritty details of why this sale? And what is the pattern of willingness for customers buying products and services?

Now, with all past data, the question is what will happen? How can I make enthrall customers? These questions had eventually transformed salesforce.com to assess the current maturity level to scale up to another dimension.

Before you embark on the transformation roadmap, I would like to present you a real-life case study of a large manufacturing company transforming the legacy I.T landscape into the digital transformational landscape. How, what they did to achieve the KPI's of digital transformation? What was their strategy? These questions will be answered as you proceed in these upcoming sections.

The client is one of the largest manufacturers of the electric locomotives, bogies etc. It's a heavy manufacturing company headquartered in Europe with offices across the globe. They had been operating in the regional operational model with several sales offices across the globe. Their employee strength was about 35,000 in total including the I.T staff, HR, and plants all inclusive. Now, this company has been delivering trains for more than 100 years with major partnerships. Therefore, their key problem statements were to consolidate, modernizing the I.T landscape, increase employee productivity and support rapid expansion in APAC and other regions globally. One of the main challenges was to keep employees constantly innovate with the changing customer outlook. Some of the problems including changing I.T landscape after the mergers and acquisitions with the main production plants supported by SAP ERP (ECC 6.0 EHP 6.0). There were over 200+ applications with many custom applications and a few standardized in SAP as a core template. However, the I.T landscape had complexities in supporting multiple standalone regional engineering and payroll applications. Because of this landscape, the maintenance costs were too high, in addition to the consulting costs. On one hand, the approach was to pursue rapid outsourcing to the India based center of excellence (COE) and on other hand is to consolidate the I.T landscape overall. Therefore, it was essential to conduct a survey of customers satisfaction across various plants geographically, who're the end-users of the core ERP application.

The customer survey results were carefully studied to conclude outcome based digital transformation. However, the company was very careful to minimize the risks and be less disruptive. It was simply not possible to disrupt the business operations in a production plant. The strategy was not deploying another platform to integrate applications; instead, the main objective was to identify customer requirements, business operation issues, and employee satisfaction. Each of the above attributes resulted in finalizing the strategy of the future digital roadmap for the organization. Though the company used SAP ECC 6.0 EHP 6.0 as a platform with Oracle database (DB) for the production activities, there were so many potential gaps identified by the business as the scope for improvements.

There were huge challenges in terms of integrating Engineering applications into ERP. The flow is like engineering product design such as CATIA, DELMIA upstream to feed manufacturing bill-of-material (BOM) via intermediate SAP system known as SAP repository and then finally goes to core SAP ERP via IDOCS (intermediate document transfers used in SAP for transformation from one system to other). The entire supply chain planning was done externally from Kinaxis tool suite and then data was fed into SAP ERP. Further adding to the complexities, the landscape was connected to the recently implemented SAP Success Factor on-cloud. This SAP HR application (Success Factor) was managed by a third-party SAP vendor supporting cloud SaaS application on the cloud. The downstream applications included manufacturing execution systems (MES) for managing shop floor production activities in the respective work center for managing operation activities. Each of the operator's activities confirmation and activity time booking was managed using complex manufacturing execution system and HR T&A tools. The data flow was between MES shop-floor with production order confirmation to the core SAP ERP where the final status of the production order is closed and cost set in the book of accounts in respective journal entries (General Ledger A/C) against respective production order.

Any organization transforming into Digital will need to be aware of the corporate political situation too. I believe not all stakeholders will be ready sign-off the approach, as they fear consequences of change. Hence, communication was important to keep all stakeholders aligned with accurate status reporting. This is one of the primary reasons that Global performance team was formed to discuss various topics related to the transformation including risks and the mitigation plan. The change management lead was responsible for conducting training across the plants, and the respective communication SPOC managed the communication across the organization. Every business functional assigned a dedicated project manager along with an end-to-end I.T project manager to manage the transformation project. The risk officer managed the risks with the mitigation plan on a regular basis. The strategic partner team supported the organization throughout the endeavor with specific skills such as business consulting, strategy and I.T skill consultants (python programming, AI architect, and project lead and integration consultant).

The leadership team was swift in completing the customer survey, consolidating pain points and made necessary bottom-up transformation in terms of HR to revamp the entire organization structure by introducing digital hub team's, thus fuelled innovation within the organization. After 2 months of initial assessment of the organization structure, the digital leader had changed the organization bottom-up by grouping IT teams into the following:

- Global performance & business partner group (this group interacts with the business regularly)

- Support functions group (For example, HR, satellite systems),

- Technology & security (I.T Infra group),

- Business solutions (Core ERP/Implementation team) & innovation groups.

- Service performance & User support (End user support group, responsible for laptops, LAN/WAN etc.)

- Integration & M&A (Overall mergers & acquisitions)

The above functions directly reported to the CIO with Digital group working as a horizontal stream across each of the above verticals. This change had totally transformed the organization into the digital organization. Each of the group performed a specific set of activities with an increased focus towards customers. For example, the business partnering team is responsible for demand management, understanding requirements and interacting closely with the customer. The business solution is responsible for I.T software implementation.

Furthermore, the story expanded with several months of grueling workshops with the business to identify critical business processes in each of the ERP streams such as:

Finance & Controlling

- Cost Centre / Company code

- Budget, forecast

- Costs (booking in respective production order, G/L account setup and cost setup) etc.

Supply Chain

- Supply Chain planning (demand/forecasts)

- Material Requirements Planning (MRP)

- Procurement (Purchase Order)

Manufacturing

- Core Manufacturing activities (PRD Order execution)

- Manufacturing Execution System

Projects & Contracts

- Establishing Project Systems (Project Network)
- Sales & distribution for managing sales (Sales Order)

Services

- Service Orders
- Post-sale services
- Maintenance, Warranty, and repair

Master data management

- Customer Master
- Material Master (HSN product #)
- Employee Master (Success Factor)
- Product Master
- Vendor Master

Big Data/Analytics

- SAP BI/BO & ClickView tools

Engineering Applications

- Design (For example Delmia, Catia & Innova)
- 3D for prototype

Portal Applications

- Employee Portal
- Supplier Portal

Interface applications

- Digital Invoice Processing (DIP)
- Thetys (Bank transfers)
- Engineering (Catia, Delmia, NEO)

These intensive workshops continued for more than six months to evolve with pain points to the business. Each of it became an opportunity for the I.T teams to collaborate across functions and implement a digital roadmap to alleviate pains of the customer. These requirements were categorized into process changes, gaps in I.T solution or change management for the business. Using agile project method for deployment, product lead came up with a product backlog. Each release was planned meticulously to deliver the changes in phases. The transformation involved I.T landscape migration to the cloud infrastructure, consolidation of applications with unified communication services for better collaboration. All the age-old customer services modules were replaced with bot based services. The changes at respective plants were interesting, such as bots to automate operations aligned with big data to identify the production activity operational excellence.

Most of the industrial equipment at the plant was enabled with IoT sensors passing back communication to ERP real time from the warehouse, storage location to the production facility. The robust tracking facility enabled logistics to perform 100% fullest to all capabilities. A traditional shop floor had transformed into a high-tech factory with IoT, AI/Big data analytics framework developed with the ERP backend support system. The change management tasks for the employees, customers were an uphill task with well-developed learning management solution (LMS) to avoid multiple sessions, as most of these sessions are standard across plants.

As we stated earlier, digital transformation is not just the process automation. It's an evolution towards newer ways of exploring the market with evolving strategies. Indeed, this was very exciting. Each of the process validation resulted in top 3 innovation along with the consolidation of the I.T landscape. Therefore, I.T leadership teams used this opportunity to build Digital Hub's across streams with required funding. Along with the integration of I.T landscape, innovating ideas were gathered based on customer pain points and survey results.

Because of the above workshops, fit & gap analysis of various processes, the digital strategy evolved a robust roadmap highlighted in Figure 3-1. The journey was challenging to the business, employees, and customer to explore various options to arrive at a common platform to collaborate, innovate better. There is no end to innovation. It is eternal as a business can grow and continue to explore more avenues. One of the interesting ideas that popped up in session became a valuable revenue making stream for the business…For example, the services were just plain in the legacy application landscape. The team worked on improving services to the customer by implementing an IoT based services. The Internet of Things (IoT) sends data from the train back to the monitor systems and core ERP. The core ERP was used as a platform to support supply chain, manufacturing, services, and execution. The enhanced application with AI/Big data platform used on the train data back to the ERP to support predictive analytics to prevent train accidents; There were many parameters analyzed such as on the train speed real-time, AI system evolved using data from the history and started building intelligent alerts to the driver.

Finally, the legacy interface landscape had transformed into AI/Big data and machine learning platform to prevent accidents. This is just one example of many innovative ideas implemented as part of the digital transformation project. Furthermore, PO/SO processes were automated to support constant business innovation, instead of spending time on trivial details. The supplier quality and performance improved gradually over a period. The company has evolved into the digital landscape with innovation hubs playing a pivotal role in the transformation processes. The I.T infra costs such as HW/SW costs have been cut-off completely by moving over to the cloud-based infrastructure and software as a service (SaaS) became the most preferred option in the digital landscape. The business groups realigned and IT landscape teams were focused and aligned with the business groups.

Thus, there was better collaboration with the innovation as the hub in the transformation story. In the end, revenue streams evolved with growing innovation in products, solutions, and services, almost in every department. The opportunities grew, markets expanded for the company with double digits growth posted in every quarter. The manufacturing plants transformed into autonomous plants using robots and the company is still energizing changes in the plant. It's an ongoing journey as I do not want to wrap up in a few words! The innovation continues in every department of the organization. The results are tangible with growing customer satisfaction, happy employees with an innovative mindset, YoY growth, expanding markets, increased sales and high-quality products and services. Of course, there were challenges in terms of aligning People, Process, and Technology with an innovative mindset.

It's a change in the mindset from just doing it to complete tasks with the digital mindset in every department. The digital leadership team was focussed over years and the business sponsor's support further helped the team to deploy changes. Though the entire endeavor was disruptive, the business as usual (BAU) operations continued without much impact, while deploying these changes. A lot of unforeseen risks escalated were controlled via a risk-mitigated approach from time to time using the agile method used in the deployment of the solution. Now, the total I.T infrastructure spending has reduced by 50% using subscription based (SaaS) delivery model and the consulting expenses had been reduced by over 70% expenses year on year (YoY). Based on the forecast, the company will achieve a full return on the investments (ROI) in less than 2 years with a break-even achieved by the 15th month.

The AI-based bots were used to automate authorization requirements. For example, password resets can be done in quick time by requesting bot for reset password. Similarly, ticket based bots were used to assign tickets to the respective teams and prioritize based on the impact. This was one of the major innovations to reduce manual overheads and cycle time reduction by 50% achieved by enabling a high level of automation. As a result, customer satisfaction improved for gaining a lot of traction to resolve key priority issues in quick turn-around. For example, "P1 (priority 1 with SLA resolution < 4 hours improved to <2)", "P2" tickets were resolved on-time.

The real challenges in the solution were to support the plant in end-to-end manufacturing operations with high-end integrated IoT controls from the warehouse to the manufacturing plants. The plant operations start from material planning and schedule (MPS) using an external interface (Kinaxis) to run requirements planning (MRP) for the supply planning.

Digital Transformation Roadmap

In the Industry 4.0 maturity models, there are several ways to look at the mentioned staged approaches. One such maturity approach looks at the information and actual operations and manufacturing systems perspective with autonomous machines and systems as true Industry 4.0.

Now, let us understand the Industry 4.0 - Digital roadmap and the stages of implementation the transformational roadmap as illustrated below in Figure 3-1 Digital Transformation Roadmap in four stages.

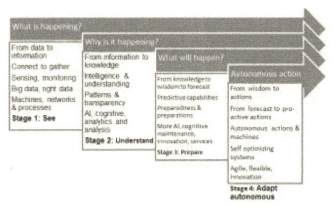

Figure 3-1 Digital Roadmap - Industry 4.0

The Industry 4.0 strategy is primarily a staged approach with value opportunities at each step and higher overall value across the journey - stages, preparations, Implementations, and actions. From the perspective of systems and equipment/machines these stages correspond with, respectively seeing what is happening (data), knowing why it's happening (analytics, knowledge), predicting what will happen (based upon the patterns and capabilities we developed before and AI) to the ultimate step Industry 4.0 strives for: an autonomous reaction by autonomous machines within the self-optimizing Industry 4.0 systems.

The second maturity approach revolves more around the business as such and corresponds with what you would typically see in any project. What do we want to achieve and what do we have today (assess), where do we want to go and what are the missing links to get there which is one of the methodological analysis in Industry 4.0, of which gap analysis is part and then the deployment of a strategic plan with a clear roadmap with regards to processes, security, skills, technologies, and implementation? And, as is always the case this is of course followed by monitoring and improvement. The building blocks of Industry 4.0: cyber-physical systems

The Cyber-physical systems (CPS) are building blocks in Industry 4.0 on one hand and part of the Industry 4.0 vision on the other. Cyber-physical systems are combinations of intelligent physical components, objects, and systems with embedded computing and storage possibilities, which get connected through networks and are the enablers of the smart factory concept of Industry 4.0 in an Internet of Things, Data, and Services scope, with a focus on processes.

In simple terms, the cyber-physical systems refer to bridging the digital (cyber) and physical entity in an industrial context. Now, let us explore the 5-stage development model in a digital transformation.

5-stage development model

The transformation from analog business to full-scale digital business can happen quickly with meticulous planning and execution. The digital enterprise must go through these five stages to a digitalized business.

- Enterprises need to master six areas in order to move from legacy to digital business by leveraging 5-stage development process. Each stage highlights the mature in business/technology vision, technology convergence, analytics and algorithms, bimodal operations, infrastructure, and organization and culture.

- First step is to find out where am I and stage your digital initiative is in, if you are pursuing the digital business at all — or perhaps your organization is running several projects at various stages

- It is important to keep a check and review the skills, tools and other resources deployed for digital transition project, and determine whether they suit the stage of digital business development.

- Initial stages of the transformation program needs more creative, agile resources who are willing to take the discussion as the opportunity arises.

- Keep an eye on the overall process and stages well in advance Look at the next stage in the development process, it is important to start the operation & Run team in terms on knowledge, Skills sets etc for smooth handover.

Typically, in most enterprises, digital business starts with a leader, who may have a narrow idea for a new product or service. However, it should end up as an enterprise wide commitment to digital business innovation at scale. Digital business is the business strategy. In order to succeed in digital business, these enterprises must go through a series of transformations to move from the first to the final stage.

Figure 3-2. Strategic Roadmap for Digital Business

Current State	Future State	Gap	Migration Plan
• Lack of clarity regarding digital business goals • Business-As-Usual (BAU) • Lack of Innovation • Lack of customer experience	• Create digital goals • Create prototype • Deliver minimum viable product • Scale up business & • Optimize key busienss processes	• Technology convergence • Bimodal operations • Infrastructure • Business vision • Analytics & algorithm • Organization & culture	• Define digital business goals • Define key performance indicators (KPI) to measure performance • Build repository of innovation examples in the respecitve line of business

It's important for enterprises to evaluate the current state and envision the future State of the digital business. In order to succeed in digital business, enterprises must cycle through five stages.

The Five Stages of Digital Business

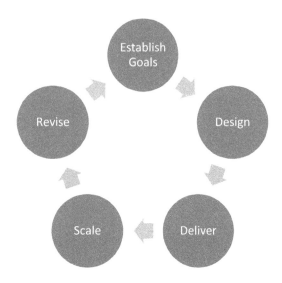

Figure 3-3. Five development stages of the digital business

Let us explore each of these stages in detail.

Stage 1: Establish Goals

First and foremost, it is important for a digital leader to establish goals. In order to instil confidence in the team, create a business moment, where people, business and technology work together to solve a problem or create value. The leaders realize they need an enterprise strategy to address how digital technologies will influence the business model and a roadmap to ensure the enterprise grows and stays relevant.

Stage 2: Design

Most digital business leaders start small steps to succeed to create a positive impact. They create one or more prototypes that will have an impact on a product or channel. For example, sensors, location awareness, advanced analytics and mobility. The prototype involves a product with a business model or industry vision supporting it. The enterprise creates a team to innovate rapidly around the new digital offering. The organization is building confidence in its ability to respond to technology disruptions.

Stage 3: Deliver

Delivery of digital services play an important component It is important to build a delivery strategy for digital business and places a seasoned team leader in charge of it. The leader need to put the best team to deploy a minimum viable product that creates a competitive advantage or new capability. A leader has to take a Bimodal approach. After testing the minimal viable product(MPV) in real world scenario, the team eventually feels confident enough to launch a pilot project and test the whole outcome end to end.

Stage 4: Scale

Once the MPV is done and pilot is successful the Leader needs to put the knowledge in practice for larger platforms involving larger IT Ecosystems and Functions. Technologies such as AR , VR & MR, smart machines, algorithms and embedded analytics replace human intervention. What is important is that once the pilot is successful the learning from stage 1 to 4 needs to been analysed and rapidly cycle through 2 to 4 many times to find a winning, scalable product. Cycling from step 1 to 4 helps find loop holes if any and scale up the project and put the learning for use on a larger platform.

Stage 5. Revise

With the continuous use of steps from stage 1 to 4 the organisation achieves digital transformation and then over a period it reaches to a point when the enterprise become digital enterprise. New revenue and profit from digital initiatives outpace those from conventional business. Revenues, profile margin and operating margin goes up. Digital transformation also helps enterprises to create an niche brand for them, look at the example of Ge they have setup whole organisation to create digital space for them which is creating a brand for GE and now GE can call themselves as Digital and they have started realising the financial benefits from the transformation and their end customers are able to realise the benefits on the product bought from GE as well. Brand equity is dramatically enhanced. The enterprise focuses on refining the digital offering and optimizing its technical and business performance.

85

KPI

The KPI will be measured by productivity of employees, by measuring cycle time reduction on number of incidents on their digitised platform and the overall revenue and profile margins generated after the digitisation is.

Assess your current State

One important aspect to understand is that the are misnomer in IT world and calling most of the things in IT World as digital, for example Many enterprises use the term "digital business" to refer to anything that uses digital technology as Digital Business. In many cases, the initiative involves executing transactions through new channels, which is more properly e-business, or engaging customers through new online channels — digital marketing (see Figure 3-4). Digital business proper involves a combination of algorithms and smart machines will start to drive digital business. Mainstream enterprises have only just started to experiment with digital technology and they cannot be called digitised. The following figure illustrates digital business evolution.

Digital Business Evolution

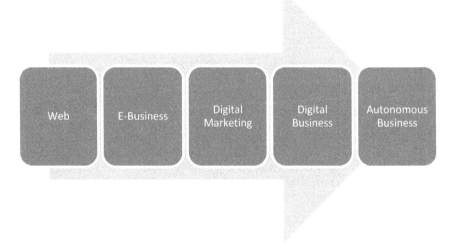

Figure 3-4. Digital business evolution

Gap Analysis and Interdependencies

Areas for enterprise to master for them to become a digital enterprise.:

- Business Technology Alignment: There are few leaders who understand the use of technology in enterprises and have visibility on application of technology for business and transformation must be involved. These few leaders may be in business units or in the IT organization. Their vision needs to be propagated across the organization.

- Technology convergence: For Digital Transformation it is important to bridge the digital and physical worlds, digital business must combine the IoT, such as sensors, wearables and smart machines.

- Extensive use of Algorithms and analytics: The whole idea of Digital business is to deliver value to customers. The enterprise will know more about customers, especially their context and intention at any moment, and will deliver unique solutions for what they most need. In order to harness the digital capability, Enterprises must improve their capabilities in analytics and algorithms to operate at this pace and complexity.

- Bimodal operations: Enterprise must operate in Bi Modal IT that is they must create MVP for a product to test and at the same time should be able to run BAU application and scale them up as part of their operation, Digital transformation requires rapid design and prototyping in the early stages, the enterprise could be scaling up one digital product and prototyping another at the same time IT Leaders must be ready to work in Agile Mode.

- Infrastructure Improvement: One key areas that IT leaders must Understand that for digital transformation Conventional IT infrastructure will not support digital business. IT Infrastructure has to handle the real-time data fast and process them quick. Leaders need to look at hyper converged infra. It must expand to incorporate the many new data types of IoT and OT. The IT infrastructure must be robust enough to handle all this data — perhaps an order of magnitude greater than data from IT systems alone.

- Team : Digital transformation is not easy to achieve In the early stages, Teams who are working on project must be protected and encouraged to work to achieve the target making sure that they are not neglected by core business Teams must be fostered and protected from established business units that may kill it out of neglect or malice the general tendency is to underestimate the digital transformation and initially there is lesser acceptance among business for transformation and they are resistance to change. Leaders must foster a spirit of openness and collaboration between teams so that people work across business and technology without silos.

Migration Plan

What is most important is for digital journey is to start, where to start is question and that is illustrated below figure (see Figure 3-5). Time may be the most important factor as Gartner's survey cited. Hence it is important for digital leaders to prioritise the project, projects that need are prioritised for business and will help achieve productivity and improve financial gains. The strategic roadmap of digital business timeline is illustrated below in Figure 3-5.

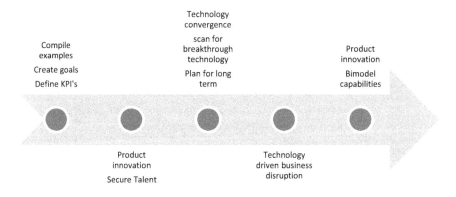

Figure 3-5. Digital business Timeline

It's important for digital leaders to prioritize tasks as high, medium and low.

High

The foremost activity for a digital leader is to create an Industry vision. Create an industry vision: An industry vision proposes nothing less than the complete redefinition of the enterprise, as well as the industry. It is one vision of many that could be possible for any given industry. The purpose of an industry vision is to stretch thinking about what is possible.

KPI: Define KPI's to identify how business activities will affect financial performance. These performance metrics enhance IT-to-business communication by allowing greater precision in addressing the complex issues around value creation in digital business.

Medium

Next, priority is to create a business moment. A business moment sets in motion a series of events and actions involving a network of people, businesses and things that spans or crosses multiple industries and multiple ecosystems.

- Nurture talent & retention plan: The Digital business requires people who combine business and technology expertise. They must be versatile, creative and collaborative, particularly in the early stages. The later stages need people who can build, integrate and scale digital business systems.
- Improve real-time analytics: Advanced analytics solves problems by diagnosing root causes and effects, and by anticipating and optimizing outcomes, behaviours, and processes. Digital business will require new analytic model and unique algorithms — and people who can build them.
- Create bimodal capability: Those supporting digital business must prepare to incorporate digital innovations into the way they operate. Marrying a more predictable evolution of products and technologies with the new and innovative is the essence of a bimodal capability.

89

Low

Imagine new industries: The Digital business will often eliminate the traditional boundaries between industries and bring markets together. The enterprise can gain new opportunities by using digital technology to create products for adjacent markets.

- **Robust architecture for technology convergence**: The IoT/OT will generate huge volume, velocity and variety of data. Enterprises must rearchitect their data management systems, adopt new data management services and platforms, and create new flow policies and practices. An IoT platform is the centrepiece. It controls the ingestion, storage and analysis of device data.
- **Identify breakthrough technologies**: New technologies will continue to emerge that create new opportunities for digital business. The enterprise needs a permanent function that evaluates new technologies for their business potential.
- **Envisage goals for long term**: A digital leader should think about the distant future as they build digital business capabilities. By 2020, algorithms will not only provide insight but will also become pivotal to competitive differentiation. We believe by the end of 2030, smart machines and algorithms will operate businesses with little or no human involvement. Algorithmic and autonomous business have implications for enterprise strategy, technology and organization.

Let's deep dive into various steps involved in the Digital Transformation strategy, now, let's explore the roadmap and how the organization had transformed.

90

Digital Transformation Steps

As you had noticed in the case study discussed, the first step is to understand the starting point of where you're right now? The following table 3-1 illustrates the assessment of P3, which indicates people, process, and technology of the current situation.

Table 3-1. P3 assessment. The following analysis would yield benefits in terms of planning and roadmap of digital transformation based on the current situation

1.   P3 assessment of the current situation in the organization as highlighted below.

Table 3-1 P3 assessment

Category	Emergent	Managed	Optimized	Transformed
People	Pioneers driven by personal interest	knowledgeable team engaged	Knowledgeable team engaged	Digital Excellence to ensure innovation, agility & responsiveness
Process	Inadequate controls and measurements	Strategic decision in silos with no global vision	Strategic decision, targets planned	
Technology	Legacy systems with several interfaces and infra overheads	Some integrated systems that are partially automated	Fully integrated systems well managed	

1. Define excellence for business

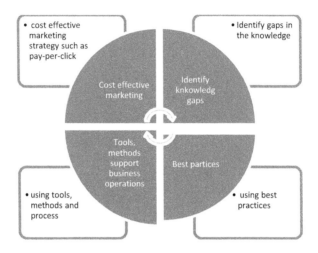

Figure 3-2 Define excellence

- People: Pioneers driven by personal interest knowledgeable team engaged
  - Knowledgeable team engaged Digital Excellence to ensure innovation, agility & responsiveness
- Process: Inadequate controls and measurements
  - Strategic decision in silos with no global vision
  - Strategic decision targets planned
- Technology: Legacy systems with several interfaces and infra overheads.
  - Some integrated systems that are partially automated
  - Fully integrated systems well managed

2. Align organization with competency frameworks as illustrated below.

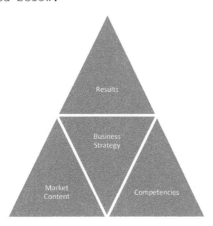

Figure 3-3 Competency Framework

3. Understand skill requirements to upgrade for the Digital Competence:

Table 3-2 Skill assessment

Skills	Process	Tools	Culture
Digital skills are very essential	Readiness of the Organization to stage process changes	Access to right digital tools & networks. Are these tools centrally managed?	Transition from hierarchy mind-set to openness with innovative mind-set

Digital Skills

- Digital skills are very essential

- Assess Readiness of the Organization to stage process changes

- Access to right digital tools & networks. Are these tools centrally managed?

A transition from hierarchy mindset to openness with an innovative mindset

- Ensure rights skills developed in the workplace and digital leadership

- Ensure senior executives understand the business environment needed and finally, what we do?

- Digital marketing is digital business

- Change isn't easy -do something different

Digital roadmap - People

As you know, the main asset of any organization is 'THE PEOPLE', employees in the organization. To build a digital organization, core aspect is to develop digital skills with leadership commitment. Perhaps, HR process, policies will need a change to build a new organization with digital culture as the core part of the strategy. This process of transformation is a time-bound process; hence you'll need to anticipate ROI over a period and not an immediate result.

Digital roadmap - Process

Now, the next step in digital transformation is to build a framework of core processes with the support of leadership. For example, digital transformation involves big data, analytics, e-commerce platforms and mobility. You may need to transform standalone customer relationship management tools (CRM) combined with unified communication and customer care services with enhanced analytics. Therefore, the process plays a vital role in shaping up a digital transformation as illustrated below digital balanced scorecard.

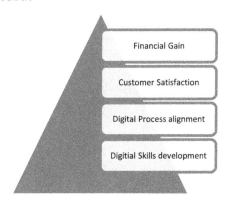

Digital Balanced scorecard

Digital Roadmap - Technology

As we defined People and Process, it is important to focus on a robust technology platform to support digital transformation strategy. It is not re-inventing a new technology, perhaps, to consolidate a robust technology platform customized for your requirements in the digital era. For example, content management systems such as LMS for enhancing learning experiences, payment enabled with PayTM kind of tools for improving customer experience. The recent survey has strongly provided user experience at the center stage. You may use IBM Watson, Microsoft Azure, Oracle Cloud platform or SAP Leonardo. The ability to transform these ERP platforms into Digital Platform combined with Artificial intelligence is the key to a successful transformation to improve customer satisfaction. In the next section, we will explore the transformational strategy.

Digital transformation Strategic view

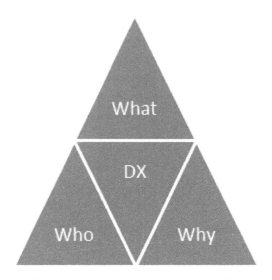

Figure 3-2 Digital Transformation Strategy View.

As illustrated in Figure 3-2 above, the first steps in deploying a Digital Transformation strategy is to ask key questions on whom? What? Why? Perhaps your organization strategy might be deploying a digital strategy in stages or the big bang. The goal of Digital transformation could be a simple automation of processes or leverage all opportunities that exist to define revised business models, revenue model etc. In some cases where digital transformation is an end-to-end endeavor, where the key performance indicator is to ensure simplified business processes, revenue model changes and utilizing capacity to the fullest. However, none of these changes can occur overnight. Your organization digital transformation journey will be measured in incremental steps. Hence, the goal is to assess tangible outcomes at regular intervals with key questions as illustrated below in Figure 3-3.

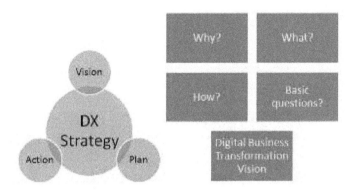

Figure 3-3 Key Digital transformation questions

Each of the above questions is very crucial to build organization strategy for transformation. Why are you doing this and what is the goal? The vision evolved will help you in the transformation journey. Further, the vision will evolve in the high-level program plan and then into sub-components of the project plan with tasks.

Digital transformation client experiences

The key driver of any Digital Transformation project is the enhanced customer experience. As illustrated in Figure 3-3, you'll need to conduct surveys to capture the voice of the customer, draw a baseline. From the baseline, you'll need to trace a progressive path to implement innovations and improvements. It's important to keep your clients engaged, employees motivated using a loyalty bonus as an innovative mindset should be appreciated to continuously improve.

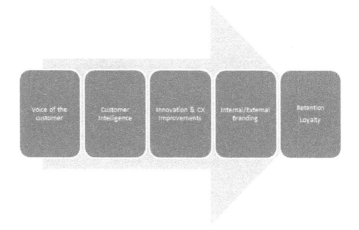

Figure 3-4 Digital Transformation client experiences

Indeed, the customer experience doesn't belong to just one department and a transformational approach includes several stakeholders, including the customer. It is true that technology has enhanced customer experiences, behavior and expectations, thus enabling transformations. The next focus is on people and processes. To truly enhance the customer experience in an enterprise-wide and holistic way, several elements, divisions, caveats, processes, and technologies need to be considered. The three key dimensions are people, process, and technology for driving Digital Transformation.

Digital transformation and marketing

As you know sales & marketing is one of the key elements of Digital Transformation. This is how you'd communicate your innovative products and services to the world. Perhaps, marketing is the first step towards demonstrated your digital initiatives to the clients. Gone are the days of marketing leads going through multiple channels to asses marketing data. It's readily available in the software packages such as CRM to understand the conversion rate of prospects to the customer. It will help organizations to assess the importance of Digital marketing methods and tools to help access data in real time. The customer expectations and consumer behavior changes, hence it is important to capture changes in a model that can relate to your products and services internally. This is how you'd be able to embark on the digital transformation journey.

Today, digital client's consumption model has changed due to the advent of e-commerce. Thus, sales and marketing function has a pivotal role in the journey of Digital Transformation with the change in the mindset of consumers, business model and the role of Digital marketing leadership to transform the organization to the next level. In summary, Digital transformation strategy will include a major role for the Digital Marketing strategies and goals. This goes together with the optimization goals of the business functions and interconnectedness of various departments within the organization. Let's look at the holistic optimization approach as illustrated in Figure 3-5 Digital Transformation Holistic optimization approach

Digital transformation and holistic optimization

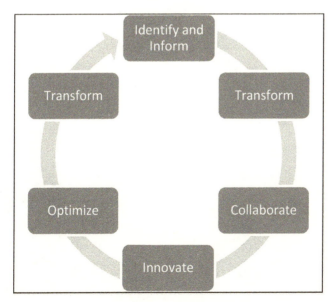

Figure 3-5 Digital transformation holistic approach

One of the main pitfalls of digital transformation projects has been the lack of a holistic approach. In most of the organizations, process automation was done in silos; hence the benefits were not tangible in terms of business process optimization and/or the optimization of SLA's with clients. The best approach is to integrate your strategy by involving partners, customers and internal key stakeholders such as employees and internal departments align to ensure everyone is aware of and contribute to the vision. Organization change management is a key activity, stakeholders must be aligned to succeed in the digital transformation endeavor with strong digital leadership. Some of the key questions and core digital transformation related to Information challenges are discussed in the next section.

Key questions to ask:

These are the key information challenges as illustrated in Figure 3-6 below:

- How do we optimize core business processes?

- How do we get valuable insights out of data?

- How do you engage clients, employee, and partners by leveraging tools, methods, and accelerators?

- How do you mitigate risks?

Now, let us analyze core digital transformation challenges:

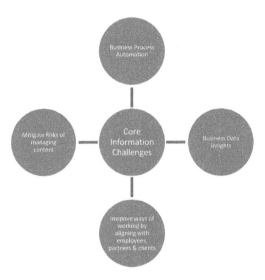

Figure 3-6 Digital transformation Challenges.

As illustrated above in Figure 3-6 there are 4 core digital transformation challenges related to the information technology. It's essential for organizations to turn these information challenges into solutions by transforming into opportunities. Information technology plays a vital role in digital transformation projects as an enabler in every step of customer focus, operational excellence and knowledge workers. Information Technology is the key enabler to integrate people, process and technology in the organization to pave way for a successful transformation journey.

Digital transformation and information management

It's important to harness data to be able to succeed in any digital transformation journey. Every organization has some form of data marts, data warehouses as powerhouses of information storage and processing. However, the key enabler of digital transformation is the way you're able to harness it to make business insights out of it. Perhaps, this is where Information technology helps you to put a process in place using machine learning to build autonomous

101

systems that can build intelligent information systems that can make decisions. This is the basic concept of AI systems that use programming such as python with API's connected to the backend systems and data warehouses to bring data into in-memory as real-time data for quick access with intelligent insights.

Furthermore, your machine learning (AI) capabilities and services can work as an autonomous system that can consolidate data, analyze and make decisions. This is an intuitive system that will transform organizations to the next level of automation to digitally transformed intelligent systems that are capable of thinking with decision-making capabilities. This is the upcoming trendsetter in every Industry and a breakthrough as we have observed the Information systems acting as enablers for decision making, however in the first time Information systems have transformed into digital organizations as autonomous systems that can make its own decisions. This is very interesting to learn and explore capabilities in many organizations.

This is exactly where AI capabilities help organizations to transform as a digital era. The advent of the Internet of Things and Web 3.0 upon us the intelligent dimension becomes more important in transforming unstructured information, automation and connected devices to work in an integrated manner for the first time in the history of Information Technology. These are intelligent systems that function as enablers to help organizations to the digital transformation. It is imperative to build intelligent systems, rather than developing information systems for digital organizations as real assets of the enterprise, an intelligent information management approach enters the boardroom. I have witnessed this evolution in SAP as it is transforming information systems into intelligent systems by focussing on harnessing data from disparate systems to in-memory platforms to make real-time decisions. Thus, it has enabled a platform for clients, employees, and partners to make quick decisions.

Furthermore, information systems are turning into intelligent systems by transforming volumes of data into insightful. This is done by collecting data from IoT devices, processed using a machine learning algorithm to build it autonomous decision-making capabilities. Thus, transforming system information landscape into intelligent information landscape encompassing IoT, AI and big data/analytics capabilities to process data available with decision-making capabilities as illustrated below in Figure 3-6 intelligent systems triangle.

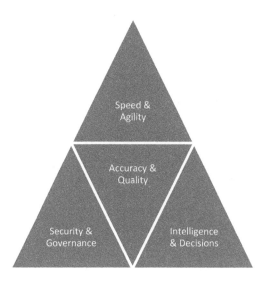

Figure 3-6 intelligent systems

The new age intelligent system is not about managing data and information in the traditional sense, however, the objective is to harness data from disparate sources and provide intelligent capabilities using AI to make decisions as autonomous systems. Hence, it is no longer Infosystems; it is transformed into intelligent systems of smart I.T systems. As illustrated in Figure 3-6, smart I.T systems provide:

- AI capabilities to harness data to the fullest potential

- Holistic security approach to protect data security and privacy

- Improved quality and outcomes

- Core business process transformation

Thus, systems are evolving into intelligent, autonomous with algorithms of cognitive computing with quick access to real-time data using in-memory computing methods. The in-memory access to data is provided by S/4HANA, which is the latest evolution of SAP. Now, let us explore the man-machine coordination, where Cyber-physical systems (CPS) collaborated with the intelligent systems.

Cyber-physical systems (CPS)

It fits more in the Operational Technology (OT) side of the converging IT/OT world which is typical in Industry 4.0 and the Industrial Internet. So, if you want to understand Industry 4.0 or the Industrial Internet, you'll need an understanding of some essential operational, production and mechanics terms.

Cyber-physical systems (CPS) in the Industry 4.0 view are based on the latest control systems, embedded software systems and an IP address (the link with the Internet of Things becomes clearer, although strictly both are not the same they certainly are twins as we see in the next 'chapter'.

In the Industry 4.0 context of mechanics, engineering and so forth, cyber-physical systems are the next stage in an evolution of an ongoing improvement of enhancement and functions integration.

Looking at Industry 4.0 as the next new stage in the organization and control of the value chain across the lifecycle of products, this ongoing improvement in which CPS fits started with mechanical systems, moved to mechatronics, where we use controllers, sensors and actuators, more terms that are familiar in IoT and ad Optronics, and is now entering this stage of extensively using cyber-physical systems.

Cyber-physical systems essentially enable us to make industrial systems capable to communicate and network them, which then adds to existing manufacturing possibilities. They result in new possibilities in areas such as structural health monitoring, track and trace, remote diagnosis, remote services, remote control, condition monitoring, systems health monitoring and so forth.

And it's with these possibilities, enabled by networked and communicating cyber-physical modules and systems, that realities such as the connected or smart factory, smart health, smart cities, smart logistics etc. are possible as mentioned previously.

Industry 4.0 building blocks

The Internet of Things (IoT) is omnipresent in Industry 4.0 and its international counterparts, as mentioned previously. As you can read on our page on the Industrial Internet of Things (IoT) and deduct from the graphic above on cyber-physical systems, CPS essentially is mainly about the Industrial Internet of Things.

Internet of Things and cyber-physical systems: similar characteristics - The presence of an IP address means that cyber-physical systems, as objects, are connected to the Internet (of Things). An IP address also means that the cyber-physical system can be uniquely identified within the network. This is a key characteristic of the Internet of Things as well. The main Internet of Things use case in manufacturing, from a spending perspective, concerns manufacturing operations

The Cyber-physical systems are also equipped with sensors, actuators and all the other elements which are part of the Internet of Things. Cyber-physical systems, just like the Internet of Things need connectivity. The exact connectivity technologies which are needed depend on the context. The Internet of Things consists of objects with embedded or attached technologies that enable them to sense data, collect them and send them for a specific purpose. Depending on the object and goal this could be capturing data regarding movement, location, presence of gasses, temperature, 'health' conditions of devices, the list is endless. This data as such is just the beginning, the real value starts when analyzing and acting upon them, in the scope of the IoT project goal.

The IoT devices can also receive data and instructions, again depending on the 'use case'. All this applies to cyber-physical systems as well, which are essentially connected objects. There are more similar characteristics but you see how much there is in common already.

CPS-enabled capabilities with IoT – use cases

Moreover, the new capabilities which are enabled by cyber-physical systems, such as structural health monitoring, track and trace and so forth are essentially what we call the Internet of Things to use cases.

In other words: what you can do with the Internet of Things. Some of them are used in a cross-industry way, beyond manufacturing. Below are two examples of CPS-enabled capabilities we tackled previously and how they really are IoT uses cases. Track and trace possibilities in practice lead to multiple IoT use cases in, among others, healthcare, logistics, warehousing, shipping, and mining and even in the consumer-oriented Internet of Things use cases. There are ample applications of the latter with numerous solutions and technologies. You can track and trace your skateboard, your pets, anything really, using IoT.

The structural health monitoring is also omnipresent, mainly across Industries such as engineering, building maintenance, facility management, etc. With the right sensors and systems, you can monitor the structural health of all kinds of objects, from bridges and objects in buildings to the production assets and cyber-physical assets in manufacturing and Industry 4.0.

Smart factories, smart plants, and smart applications

The new capabilities, of which we just mentioned two and which are possible thanks to CPS in the Industry 4.0 view, in turn, enable smart plants, smart factories and anything smart. What is a core enabler of smart logistics and so forth? Indeed, the (Industrial) Internet of Things, beyond its simple aspects of sensors, actuators, communication capabilities and data collection/analytics. You can perfectly compare this with the Internet of Everything view of connected objects, people, processes and data as the building blocks of smart applications.

IoT and Industry 4.0 connectivity

A key component of the Industrial Internet of Things is connectivity. According to research, industrial manufacturers still have some catching up to do in regards with connectivity overall.

Among others, the adoption of cloud-based services and the connection of legacy systems to digital networks are lagging somewhat behind. Yet, as IoT strategies are being envisioned and designed, the number of Industrial Internet of Things connections is growing rapidly and changes occur in the types of connectivity solutions that are used.

In 2017 research from ABI Research, it is estimated that in 2017 there will be 13 million extra (new) wireline and wirelines connections across the globe. In total this would bring the number of Industrial IoT connections to 66 million. In the years after, this growth continues and even accelerates (18 million new connections per year by 2021).

Looking at the various types of Industrial IoT connection solutions in manufacturing and thus Industry 4.0, it is expected that revenues from cellular and satellite connectivity fees will reach more than $138 million in 2017.

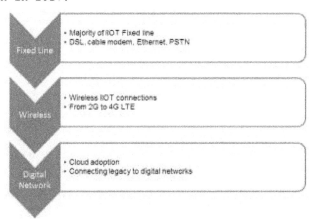

Figure 1-5 Industry 4.0 and IIOT connections

The major part of connections consists of fixed-line deployments but wireless is growing and will account for approximately a quarter of all new connections in 2017. Moreover, in the longer term, it is expected that LPWA will be the fastest grower and that the shift to 4G LTE continues.

While, as mentioned the Industrial Internet Consortium has a framework, called IIRA (Industrial Internet Reference Architecture), German 'Platform Industry 4.0' developed the so-called Reference Architectural Model Industry 4.0 (RAMI 4.0).

Industry 4.0 RAMI 4.0

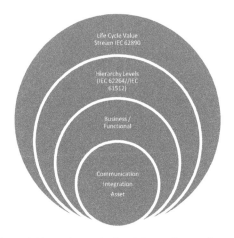

RAMI 4.0, although originating from Germany, just as Industry 4.0, is playing an increasing role in other countries as well. Even if some EU countries use different terms such as an intelligent factory, future industry, digital production or smart manufacturing, the European Commission (EC) is also involved.

The 3-dimensional RAMI 4.0 model as illustrated above shows the production object must be tracked across its entire lifecycle. Early 2017, a forum was held in the scope of the EC's 'Digitizing European Industry' project. Industry 4.0 and RAMI 4.0 are also clearly mentioned within various programs on the website of the EC (and a PDF with the essence of the Reference Architectural Model Industry 4.0 is available on it, not without reason).

At the mentioned forum, the so-called 'Stakeholder Forum', held in early 2017, international collaboration around Industry 4.0 was one of the topics. 'Platform Industry 4.0' used the occasion to further expand bilateral relationships with, among others the French Industry of the Future Alliance (Alliance Industry du Future) and Italy's

Intelligent Factory project. Outside of the EU, partners include the mentioned Industrial Internet Consortium (IIC) and Japan's Robot Revolution Initiative (meanwhile, Japan announced its all-encompassing Society 5.0 initiative at the CeBIT 2017 tradeshow). An overview of the ongoing acceptance and leverage of Industry 4.0 technologies, concepts, and principles, as mentioned previously, at the bottom of this page with over a dozen Industry 4.0 initiatives across the globe

The life cycle and value stream dimension

The life cycle and value stream dimension, as the term already describes, covers the various data mapping stages across relevant life cycles in RAMI 4.0 and across the entire value chain and the various processes (and stakeholders).

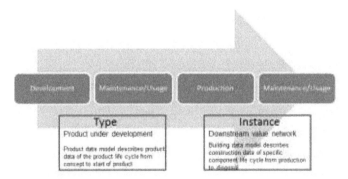

Figure 2-1 Industry 4.0 – RAMI 4.0 model – The life cycle and value stream dimension

We'll cover this more in depth later as it's key in the data part, starting from the pre-production development product data model, starting at the idea and development (data on, among others, all the way across further stages downstream, including actual production and the various processes until the production object is end of life and gets recycled or trashed). The idea: the more data early on, the more value later.

Innovation for Digital Disruption

How they operate takes a complete shift from their traditional style of operation to completely modern and technology-oriented ways the transitions referred to as Digital Transformation or disruption

Since change is the only thing constant, digital transformation has become important for all businesses, small, medium-large. Be it manufacturing, retail, consumer goods, Logistics, Financial, or high-tech industry such as IT Services automation, or medical — digital transformation is omnipresent. Delivering an excellent digital business experience to customers and employees requires the use of the of-of new innovative business application.

In the next few sections, we will uncover the concept of innovation and disruption in digital transformation and take cite some examples where the innovation has led to a massive shift in how the company operates and at the time has led to massive disruption.

These large enterprises should be able to deliver custom applications at the speed of ideas. That's the way to stay ahead in competition in today's world. Lowering operational costs and enhancing customer experience is the core of digital transformation.

Therefore, Digital transformation is not just about embracing new technology; it is about a change in thought and organization culture. There is a need for organizations to address the change in business scenarios, dynamic business demands and innovate ways to quickly cater to these changing needs. Leaders and IT teams in any enterprise should work hand in hand to meet the business requirements, drive innovation and march towards continuous improvement. This is what Digital transformation is all about — accelerates business activities, lower cost, improve time to market, and bring about a positive change in processes, people, and competency models.

The Digital transformation is also sometimes referred to as business transformation. In fact, some prefer to use the term digital business transformation, which is more in sync with the business aspect of the transformation.

Digital business transformations are driven by key factors like Innovative Technology, consumer customer behavior and market demand, and environmental factors.

Furthermore, technological innovations lead to technology disruptions. The business process moves away from legacy systems to adopt modern technology like a cloud. Big data, IoT, RAD etc. These and many such technology innovations are then used and acknowledged enterprise-wide. They bring value to the business, increase speed, lower effort and cost and deliver results more effectively.

The next factor is customer behavior. What are the customer demands and expectations of the business (and the demands on technology to meet business needs)? Customers demand increased technological capabilities combined with the desire for ease of use. And finally, organizations have a deal with external influences such as regulatory laws, changing the economy, market competition, and business partner demands.

What the customer demands and whether the technology changes can cater to the business demand is of manifold importance. Increased capabilities and lower cost are important in this. A Forrester Consulting research study done by Accenture Interactive found that the key drivers of digital transformation are profitability, customer satisfaction, and increased speed-to-market. For a successful digital transformation in any business organization, digital maturity and a modern organization culture are of paramount importance. Let's see in detail

- **Customer Demands:** Providing customers with a delightful experience in every aspect of delivery. Gain customer loyalty in a way that customers speak of your brand.

- **Process Orientation:** Process digitization and employee enablement that promotes data-driven decision-making resulting in greater performance improvement and overall operational transparency.

- **Innovation in Business:** New digital products and/or digitizing existing business models that go beyond existing business needs and foster new innovative products and service and caters to changing business needs.

The Digital Business Transformation is the real change that is causing a storm in the business world. Its impact is felt not only in operations but also in industry structures and at all levels in the organization. Business leaders and CIOs are coming forward to ensure that digital transformation coupled with innovation is driving business and bringing in productive changes and delivering value. In the next section, we will evaluate three major case studies of success Digital Transformation journey across Industry.

The key objective of Digital transformation is to achieve enhanced customer experience, operational excellence in the core business process and revenue stream business model.

What is the digital twin?

A digital twin is a software construct that bridges physical systems and the digital world. Think about it as software being paired with an instrumented physical object (or system or machine). The digital twin will be able to act as a proxy to the digital world. Digital twin will in real time accumulates data over time about the structure of the system, its operation, and the environment in which it operates. Together with the data, intelligence is built on top using analytics, physics, and machine learning. You can query the digital twin of a specific system and ask about past and present performance and operations, and ask for early warnings and predictions.

What is the outcome expected from a digital twin?

Let's be clear, digital twins are not mere twin replica t models. They are built for specific outcomes. We first think about the desired outcome--a specific key performance indicator (KPI) to ensure a specific quality of service, Digital twin help in predictive maintenance, when we talk about transformation is a journey that includes how to help and benefit customers in long run in minimizing the downtime of the product they are using, hence digital twin is a step in that direction, this is used for predictive maintenance or a prediction on the life of a specific part in order to minimize downtime, etc.—and then we figure out the bundle of data and intelligence that needs to be built in both the physical machine and the digital replica, to deliver that outcome.

Such kind of predictive analysis is important, that will help the companies take an advantage over its customers, and in long run, the customers who are buying products need to run the products for the long duration with minimum downtime to recover their operational costs and predictive analysis and maintenance can help them recover that.

A digital twin is used for predictive monitoring, diagnostics to optimize asset performance and increase the asset utilization over a longer period of time. In this field, sensory data can be combined with historical data, human expertise and on hands fleet and simulation learning to improve the outcome of prognostics. Complex System platforms like an aircraft engine, and wind turbine and bullet train can leverage the use of digital twins in finding the root cause of issues and improve productivity

The Digital twins start with data, data is the core, and hence no doubt it is said that data is the new oil, more you refine better information you get, data is valuable like oil and refining data lead to better value, & outcomes the asset model, the sensors and actuators data, as well as very broad context data and knowledge that is related to the design, building, operation and servicing of the physical twin. Analytics is the brain of the digital twin. Intelligence is built on top of the data using analytics, physics, and algorithms or machine learning. The digital twins live on a platform, which ensures persistence of the digital twin, pairing between the digital and physical twins, and creates a learning system to continuously improve the fidelity of the digital twins it hosts. Finally, the apps deliver the ultimate outcome by consuming the value generated by the digital twin, usually using APIs to query the digital twin.

Has built a world-class platform called Predix platform on which the Digital Twin and business applications run, and now is a proven industrial platform already serving the customer with predictive analysis and maintenance. Cloud capabilities are closely integrated with an on-premise Predix Machine and Edge Analytics Control System, responsible for collecting, formatting and sending machine data and for executing machine level analytics where real-time responses are required on site. Predix is specifically designed for massive data ingestion, housing and executing analytic models, managing time-series machine data and high-speed application execution. The environment, from Supervisory Control and Data Acquisition (SCADA) systems through Predix Machine to cloud and back is a highly secured environment.

Digital Transformation - case studies

Google

Let's take an example how Google has expanded its product landscape in last few years from being a search engine company they have move to chrome browser, Chrome OS, Android OS, Google Nexus, Cloud service and many more apps that are available to the user, this enables them to bind a larger customer base and provide the services that are required by the ever-changing customer base. Google is using the SMAC to change the experience of its customer and expand its user's base.

It is important that firm's organizational structure and culture must support digital transformation, with structures, governance, and incentives that promote speed, risk-taking, and experimentation—rather than kill disruptive projects before they bear fruit.

Siemens

Now, let's take an example of larger how European business Conglomerate the way they are using the digital technology for predictive maintenance which helps in rectifying the issues is handled well in advance with a minimum downtime, to tap the potential of digitalization, Siemens will use the possibilities of the digital world to improve its hardware products for the benefit of customers. With digital services such as predictive maintenance, for example, Siemens minimizes service-related downtimes for its customers. With this approach, an availability of over 99 percent has been achieved for the Madrid-Barcelona train connection, enabling the operators to impress their customers with outstanding punctuality.

The digital transformation encompasses all businesses, from power plant technology to electrification and automation through self-learning programs to self-diagnostics and condition-based maintenance. A good example of this is gas turbines in which hundreds of sensors measure temperatures, pressures, flows, and gas compositions. If these values are properly analyzed with the help of intelligent algorithms, we can give power plant operators recommendations on making more efficient settings for their plants and reducing emissions. The result is true added value – whether to conserve energy, make operations more environmentally friendly, reduce costs, accelerate processes, or increase the reliability of plants.

The company's goal is to digitize and strengthen customer relationships across channels to develop a simpler and more personal relationship with the brand. The other example is GE, a big business brand across manufacturing vertical Siemens is also working intensively on other digital technologies. These include cloud computing – which makes it possible to implement products and services faster, more cost-efficiently and at lower risk – and implementation of the Internet of Things as well as associated concepts for its industrial application. Though security is a concern that products are often deployed in critical infrastructures, IT security is written largely at Siemens.

GE

GE is using Digital twin to create a replica of physical equipment to that in digital for real-time monitoring and predictive maintenance

BFSI

The Digital Transformation in banking and financial sector is at disruptive stage from being brick and mortar banks to a digital banks, where a user is least bothered about his breach and can perform all the transaction over his digital platform or more conveniently over the mobile in safe and secure manner, now this a challenge, banks have been traditionally operating in a brick and mortar building and sudden change will need a huge amount of budget and willpower, but is there any other option available for the banks, I must say no there isn't an option available, banks have to change, but with their legacy systems and out of dated technology platforms is this possible? Remain a big question; moreover, security is a serious concern.

It is going to be a vital change in how banks and other financial institutions interact with and satisfy customers. In the end, it is the customer who ae the core, an effective Digital Transformation begins with an understanding of digital customer behavior, preferences, choices, likes, dislikes, stated as well as unstated needs, aspirations etc. And this transformation leads to the major changes in the organizations, from product-centric to customer-centric view.

A study by CGI entitled, Understanding Financial Consumers in the Digital Era sheds some light on the desires of today's digital consumer. Interestingly, at a time when financial institutions seem to be in a lock-step with each other, consumers are raising the bar on their expectations. And, according to the study customers are willing to leave their bank and move to other banks offering digital service if their needs are not met. The most effective way to understand and bring the organization from traditional banking to digital banking is Omni-Channel approach. Omni-channel is a multichannel approach to customer service where all the channels are tightly integrated, keeping the customer at the center of the integration.

As customers continue to change their channel usage patterns, banks and credit firms need to focus on delivering a seamless customer experience across various touch points. Multi-channel is a prospect to gain insights from customer's behavior preferences etc. With time being valued commodity customer are become tech savvy and do not want to spend time traveling to the banks, every customer expects a unique experience from banks. They want the banks to understand their unstated needs as well as their likes. From researching new services, opening an account, checking balance, conducting transactions, loans, credits, wealth management, customer support, and experience has become a key to success in this competitive marketplace.

Don't you think digital transformation will help to reach the banks to farthest corners of the world, I see the digital journey of banks as unique, and they will not only provide a unique customer experience but will save a huge amount of operating budget by closing their physical banks and bring in more and more customer on their digital platform. For example, Kotak Mahindra bank announced 811 savings accounts and fingerprint authentication, which is a digital account and it is easy to start within 2 minutes.

Summary

In this chapter, you've studied the Digital Transformation Strategy with case studies across various sectors with challenges observed. Also, we discussed in detail about the concept of RAMI model and high-level Implementation of transforming your Organization to the Digital World.

Industry 4.0 – Digital Transformation will transform your organization to the next evolution of standards set by the Industry. Your factories will no longer be plain shop-floors of mass productions. Instead, these factories will transform into revolutionary smart factories using robotics, IoT, cloud, big data analytics to communicate to the Operational technology. Thus, by combining the power of mobility, cyber physical applications into next generation smart factories and its benefits.

In the next chapter, let us explore evolution of Digital Transformation economy (DX).

■   ■   ■

Chapter 4: Digital Transformation Economy (DX)

The objective of this chapter is to present with artifacts of real-time transformation to successful digital transformation (DX) economy of large enterprises. This would help organizations to prepare and transform into global Industry 4.0 standards.

Now, let's understand how to make customers happy? Perhaps, you may need to re-work on strategy, development of new competencies, agile, people-oriented, innovative, customer-centric, streamlined, efficient and able to leverage opportunities to change the status quo and tap into new information –and service-driven revenues.

With the advent of big data and analytics, it is possible to analyse data from varied social media such as Facebook, LinkedIn, Pinterest, blogs or any other platform to build meaningful analytic capabilities for departments such as sales, marketing, customer services data analysis or production data analysis to analyse customer requirements closely and build long-lasting relationship. It is not a wonder to see the shop-floors changing to the state-of-art facilities with robotics. Each of these would yield details about newer opportunities that exist. Furthermore, capabilities of devices talking to each other with IoT and artificial intelligence have transformed the ancient shop floor environment to high technology oriented robotics. The invasion of GPS technology has further transformed into driverless cars, trains, and airplanes.

You've constantly updated yourself about the IoT tags provided by Samsung. These connect tags can help you in identifying many things such as your safety tags or voice recognition for operating simple home-devices etc. Let's explore the DX economy.

Evolution of digital transformation to DX economy

As we discussed about the 3rd Technology platform as the enabler for innovation accelerators as part of the digital transformation as illustrated below in Figure 4-1;

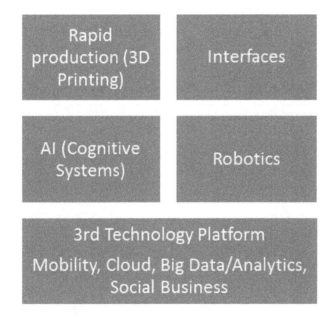

Figure 4-1 Digital transformation accelerators

The innovation accelerator is part of the core technology known as the 3rd Platform of digital transformation. The key objective is to provide enhanced digital customer experience, stakeholder experience. In addition to the above, organizations do focus on the optimization of the key business process, newer revenue models, and lower operational costs etc. With continuous improvements and innovation to demonstrate competitive differentiation, thus, digital transformation is set to become the cornerstone of a digital transformation or DX economy.

There is a possibility to extend more technologies to the 3rd Platform, thus it provides a layer of flexibility and innovation. In other words, while the core technology layer remains, the above layer of innovation provides flexibility to add more innovative products, extend to the IoT/AI devices etc. As such transformation and innovation can be accelerated. This change would eventually to a DX economy. But the bottom line is to provide digital customer experience and stakeholder experiences or the human dimension, empowered by processes, information and the 3rd Platform evolutions in the first place. You'll be able to comprehend that digital business transformation is not just a technology as it is a complete transformation. Let's explore the critical stages in transformation to DX economy.

Critical 5 stages of transformation to DX economy

As we discussed, digital technologies are not just the information technology, instead it is smart technology with abundant capabilities for innovation. Let's explore the evolution of digital transformation economy as illustrated in Figure 4-2 below.

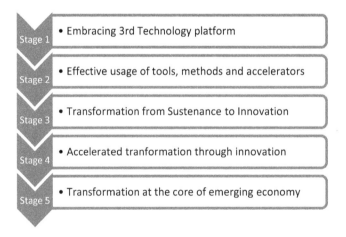

- Stage 1: • Embracing 3rd Technology platform
- Stage 2: • Effective usage of tools, methods and accelerators
- Stage 3: • Transformation from Sustenance to Innovation
- Stage 4: • Accelerated tranformation through innovation
- Stage 5: • Transformation at the core of emerging economy

- Stage 1:

Transforming legacy to the 3rd technology platform; this transformation comprises of change strategies to enable digital business which comprise of technology pillars such as cloud, big data/analytics, SMAC (social, mobile, analytics and cloud) and mobility. The rate of adoption by consumers, employees, and business with changing behavior will fuel digital realization.

- Stage 2:

Effective adoption of Tools, Methods, and accelerators of the 3rd technology platform, which predominantly includes usage of robotics in the industry, interfaces, 3D printing technology for rapid prototyping

- Stage 3: Transformation from sustenance to Innovation

It is important for companies to implement changes with long-term vision and roadmap. As discussed earlier, with newer ways of working with clients, employees, and partners. Thus, creating newer business models of revenue by forming strategy, culture, and vision to transform your business to digital reality; by continuous improvement planning, enhanced digital customer experience, automation and optimization are the key business drivers towards digital transformation.

- Stage 4: Accelerated transformation through innovation

These changes would obviously disrupt your current business model and ways of working. You'll be in a stage where the impact of digital transformation will be realized in every part of the business and IT operations. The only way to secure a successful transformation is by driving top-down with strong leadership and employee empowerment.

- Stage 5: Digital transformation at the core of an emerging economy

The digital transformation is leading us to the digital transformation economy or DX economy. This indicates digital transformation will play the pivotal role in the emerging economy with innovation strategies. Indeed, this change would impact all industries with the advent of IoT, Cognitive systems (AI) with 3rd technology platform as discussed in earlier chapters.

Acceleration of innovation and transformation

While a range of technologies has accelerated disruption, business innovation and changes in human behavior, the exponential growth and pace of change is just a fraction of what is yet to come.

Although digital business transformation is not about digital technologies as such, the adoption and opportunities of technologies under the umbrellas of social business, cloud, mobility, Big Data (analytics), cognitive computing and the Internet of Things and more will always speed up changes across society.

However, the real acceleration happens when the acceleration of innovation and transformation as such goes exponential. And that is what analysts mean when they talk about the digital transformation economy or DX economy: not just acceleration of disruption and changes but an acceleration of the actual digital transformations and innovations leading organizations will go through, making the gap with laggards even bigger as illustrated below in 4-1 Current state of I.T Landscape.

- Complex, Legacy IT systems leading to integration issues
- Manual process leading to high turn-around time in business process
- Silo data sources

Current State

- High costs
- Lack of Agility
- Lack of customer satisfaction

Impact

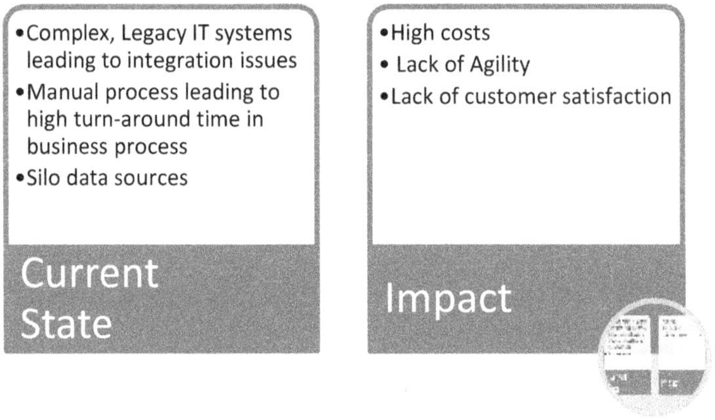

Figure 4-1 Current state of I.T Landscape

The Digital transformation projects require several elements to succeed and digitization is a part of it. Among the many elements, we mention four that are related to technology, people and/or processes.

Change management

As it is the case in virtually all impactful changes that affect multiple stakeholders, divisions, processes and technologies (including implementing an enterprise-wide marketing ROI approach, a content marketing strategy or an integrated marketing approach with CRM, marketing automation, etc. to mention three marketing-related ones), there is not only an opportunity for change and looking at what can be done better and what should be (re)connected but also a need for change management.

Knowing the role of data and analytics in digital transformation, there are even more opportunities for change and needs for change management. This is not new: when web analytics became popular, for instance, their implementation and the connection between different data and analytics "silos" in the customer/marketing space often showed clear needs for digital transformation in many customer-facing and customer-oriented operations, long before the term digital transformation became known. Grasp those opportunities and tackle the challenges. People and processes.

However, change management first and foremost obviously is about the human dimension: internal customers, stakeholders, and the broader ecosystem within which organizations reside. No organization, business, government or NGO, can realize a profound digital transformation without putting people first and have people on board. If things change too fast for people or we are not considering the individuals that are touched, as well as their concerns, this can be a recipe for failure and at a broader scale even resistance.

Priorities

The world is full of roadmaps for virtually any digital transformation project. However, roadmaps are what they are and the intent, priorities, pain points and actual needs of the individual business and the people in its ecosystem, within a broader reality, matters more.

There is never a one size fits all solution and intent, outcomes and priorities steer the digital transformation efforts, on top of changing parameters in the ecosystem. Priorities also mean prioritization, often including looking at the low hanging fruit but always with the next steps and ultimate goals in mind, knowing these goals – and the context within which they were set – will evolve.

Digitization

We mentioned it before but it's important. It's a mistake to think that organizations are ready for profound digital transformation in a broad way.

There are still far too many gaps regarding the digitization (and automation) of existing processes and the digitization of data from paper carriers. Worse: what is sometimes called digital transformation is sometimes "just" digitization (turning paper into electronic information into processes). You need digitization to optimize in a digital transformation context but digitization does not equal digital transformation. What matters is the combination, strategic and prioritized interconnecting and the actions you take to achieve business goals through digitization and combining data.

Furthermore, there is an even bigger gap between back-office processes and the front end. An example of this phenomenon can be seen in the financial industry, where there are extremely strong disconnects between the back-office and front end. There are lots and lots of digitization efforts that still need to be done in many areas of business and society and we all know and feel it, whether it's in our daily experiences as "business people" or in the often totally unnecessary administrative tasks regarding our government-related or finance-related 'duties' and interactions with business where we're forced to use paper, the phone or channels we really don't want to use anymore.

Case study

Consider an insurance company in which the CEO and her top team have reconvened following a recent trip to Silicon Valley, where they went to observe the forces reshaping their business. The team has seen how technology companies are exploiting data, virtualizing infrastructure, reimagining customer experiences, and seemingly injecting social features into everything. Now it is buzzing with new insights, new possibilities, and new threats.

The team's members take stock of what they've seen and who might disrupt their business. They make a list including not only many insurance start-ups but also, ominously, tech giants such as Google and Uber—companies whose driverless cars, command of data, and reimagined transportation alternatives could change the fundamentals of insurance. Soon the team has charted who needs to be monitored, what partnerships need to be pursued, and which digital initiatives need to be launched.

Just as the team's members begin to feel satisfied with their efforts, the CEO brings the proceedings to a halt. "Hang on," she says. "Are we sure we really understand the nature of the disruption we face? What about the next 50 start-ups and the next wave of innovations? How can we monitor them all? Don't we need to focus more on the nature of the disruption we expect to occur in our industry rather than on who the disruptors are today? I'm pretty sure most of those on our list won't be around in a decade, yet by then we will have been fundamentally disrupted. And how do we get ahead of these trends so we can be the disruptors, too?"

This discussion resembles many we hear from management teams thoughtful about digital disruption, which is pushing them to develop a view of the deeper forces behind it. An understanding of those forces, combined with solid analysis, can help explain not so much which companies will disrupt a business as for why—the nature of the transformation and disruption they face rather than just the specific parties that might initiate them.

In helping executives to answer this question, we have—paradoxically, perhaps, since digital "makes everything new"—returned to the fundamentals of supply, demand, and market dynamics to clarify the sources of digital disruption and the conditions in which it occurs. We explore supply and demand across a continuum: the extent to which their underlying elements change. This approach helps reveal the two primary sources of digital transformation and disruption. The first is the making of new markets, where supply and demand changeless. But in the second, the dynamics of hyperscaling platforms, the shifts are more profound (exhibit). Of course, these opportunities and threats aren't mutually exclusive; new entrants, disruptive attackers, and aggressive incumbents typically exploit digital dislocations in combination.

We have been working with executives to sort through their companies' situations in the digital space, separating realities from fads and identifying the threats and opportunities and the biggest digital priorities. (For a quick guide to assessing your organization's situation, see "How vulnerable are you to digital disruption?" [PDF-

57KB].) Think of our approach as a barometer to provide an early measure of your exposure to a threat or to a window of opportunity—a way of revealing the mechanisms of digital disruption at their most fundamental. It's designed to enable leaders to structure and focus their discussions by peeling back hard-to-understand effects into a series of discrete drivers or indicators they can track and help indicate the level of urgency they should feel about the opportunities and threats.

Realigning markets

We usually start the discussion at the top of the framework. In the zone to the upper right, digital technology makes accessible, sources of supply that were previously impossible to provide. In the zone to the upper left, digitization removes distortions in demand, giving customers more complete information and unbundling (or, in some cases, re-bundling) aspects of products and services formerly combined (or kept separate) by necessity or convenience or to increase profits.

The newly exposed supply, combined with newly undistorted demand, gives new market makers an opportunity to connect consumers and customers by lowering transaction costs while reducing information asymmetry. Airbnb has not constructed new buildings; it has brought people's spare bedrooms into the market. In the process, it uncovered consumer demand—which, as it turns out, always existed—for more variety in accommodation choices, prices, and lengths of stay. Uber, similarly, hasn't placed orders for new cars; it has brought onto the roads (and repurposed) cars that were underutilized previously while increasing the ease of getting a ride. In both cases, though little has changed in the underlying supply-and-demand forces, equity-market value has shifted massively: At the time of their 2015 financing rounds, Airbnb was reported to be worth about $25 billion and Uber more than $60 billion.

Airbnb and Uber may be headline-making examples, but established organizations are also unlocking markets by reducing transaction costs and connecting supply with demand. Major League Baseball has deployed the dynamic pricing of tickets to better reflect (and connect) supply and demand in the primary market for tickets to individual games. StubHub and Seat Geek do the same thing in the secondary market for tickets to baseball games and other events.

Let's take a closer look at how this occurs.

Today's consumers are widely celebrated for their newly empowered behaviors. By embracing technology and connectivity, they use apps and information to find exactly what they want, as well as where and when they want it— often for the lowest price available. As they do, they start to fulfill their own previously unmet needs and wants. Music lovers might always have preferred to buy individual songs, but until the digital age, they had to buy whole albums because that was the most valuable and cost-effective way for providers to distribute music. Now, of course, listeners pay Spotify a single subscription fee to listen to individual tracks to their hearts' content.

Similarly, with photos and images, consumers no longer must get them developed and can instead process print, and share their images instantly. They can book trips instantaneously online, thereby avoiding travel agents, and binge-watch television shows on Netflix or Amazon rather than wait a week for the next installment. In category after category, consumers are using digital technology to have their own way.

In each of these examples, that technology alters not only the products and services themselves but also the way customers prefer to use them. A "purification" of demand occurs as customers address their previously unmet needs and desires—and companies uncover underserved consumers. Customers don't have to buy the whole thing for the one bit they want or to cross-subsidize other customers who are less profitable to companies.

Skyrocketing customer expectations amplify the effect. Consumers have grown to expect best-in-class user experiences from all their online and mobile interactions, as well as many offline ones. Consumer experiences with any product or service—anywhere—now shape demand in the digital world. Customers no longer compare your offerings only with those of your direct rivals; their experiences with Apple or Amazon or ESPN are the new standard. These escalating expectations, which spill over from one product or service category to another, get paired with a related mindset, amid a growing abundance of free offerings, customers are increasingly unwilling to pay, particularly for information-intensive propositions. (This dynamic is as visible in business-to-business markets as it is in consumer ones.) In short, people are growing accustomed to having their needs fulfilled at places of their own choosing, on their own schedules, and often gratis. Can't match that? There's a good chance another company will figure out how.

What, then, are the indicators of potential disruption in this upper-left zone, as demand becomes less distorted? Your business model may be vulnerable if any of these things are true:

- Your customers must cross-subsidize other customers.

- Your customers must buy the whole thing for the one bit they want.

- Your customers can't get what they want where and when they want it.

- Your customers get a user experience that doesn't match global best practice.

When these indicators are present, so are opportunities for digital transformation and disruption. The mechanisms include improved search and filter tools, streamlined and user-friendly order processes, smart recommendation engines, the custom bundling of products, digitally enhanced product offerings, and new business models that transfer economic value to consumers in exchange for a bigger piece of the remaining pie.

Exposing new supply

On the supply side, digitization allows new sources to enter product and labor markets in ways that were previously harder to make available. As "software eats the world"—even in industrial markets—companies can liberate supply anywhere under-utilized assets exist. Airbnb unlocked the supply of lodging. Alibaba uses crowdsourcing to connect with formerly unreachable sources of innovation. Amazon Web Services provides an on-the-fly scalable infrastructure that reduces the need for peak capacity resources. Number26, a digital bank, replaces human labor with digital processes. In these examples and others like them, new supply becomes accessible and gets utilized closer to its maximum rate.

What are the indicators of potential disruption in this upper-right zone as companies expose previously inaccessible sources of supply? You may be vulnerable if any of the following things are true:

- Customers use the product only partially.

- Production is inelastic to price.

- Supply is utilized in a variable or unpredictable way.

- Fixed or step costs are high.

These indicators let attackers disrupt by pooling redundant capacity virtually, by digitizing physical resources or labor, and by tapping into the sharing economy.

Emerging market

Any time previously unused supply can relate to latent demand, market makers have an opportunity to come in and make a match, cutting into the market share of incumbents—or taking them entirely out of the equation. In fact, without the market makers, unused supply and latent demand will stay outside of the market. Wikipedia famously unleashed latent supply that was willing and elastic, even if unorganized, and unbundled the product so that you no longer had to buy 24 volumes of an encyclopedia when all you were interested in was, say, the entry on poodles. Google's AdWords lowers search costs for customers and companies by providing a free search for information seekers and keyword targeting for paying advertisers. And iFixit makes providers' costs more transparent by showing teardowns of popular electronics items.

To assess the vulnerability of a given market to new kinds of market makers, you must (among other things) analyze how difficult transactions are for customers. You may be vulnerable if you have any of these:

- high information asymmetries between customers and suppliers

- high search costs

- fees and layers from intermediaries

- long lead times to complete transactions

Attackers can address these indicators through the real-time and transparent exchange of information, disintermediation, and automated transaction processing, as well as new transparency through search and comparison tools, among other approaches.

Extreme shifts

The top half of our matrix portrays the market realignment that occurs as matchmakers connect sources of new supply with newly purified demand. The lower half of the matrix explains more extreme shifts—sometimes through new or significantly enhanced value propositions for customers, sometimes through reimagined business systems, and sometimes through hyper-scale platforms at the center of entirely new value chains and ecosystems. Attacks may emerge from adjacent markets or from companies with business objectives completely different from your own so that you become "collateral damage." The result can be not only the destruction of sizable profit pools but also the emergence of new control points for value.

Established companies relying on existing barriers to entry—such as high physical-infrastructure costs or regulatory protection—will find themselves vulnerable. User demand will change regulations, companies will find collaborative uses for expensive infrastructure, or other mechanisms of disruption will come into play.

Companies must understand many radical underlying shifts in the forces of supply and demand specific to each industry or ecosystem. The power of branding, for example, is being eroded by the social validation of a new entrant or by consumer scorn for an incumbent. Physical assets can be virtualized, driving the marginal cost of production toward zero. And information is being embedded in products and services so that they themselves can be redefined.

Taken, these forces blur the boundaries and definitions of industries and make more extreme outcomes a part of the strategic calculus.

New and enhanced value propositions

As we saw in the top half of our framework, purifying supply and demand means giving customers what they always wanted but in new, more efficient ways. This isn't where the disruptive sequence ends, however. First, as markets evolve, the customers' expectations escalate. Second, companies meet those heightened expectations with new value propositions that give people what they didn't realize they wanted and do so in ways that defy conventional wisdom about how industries make money.

Few people, for example, could have explicitly wished to have the Internet in their pockets—until advanced smartphones presented that possibility. In similar ways, many digital companies have gone beyond improving existing offerings, to provide unprecedented functionality and experiences that customers soon wanted to have. Giving consumers the ability to choose their own songs and bundle their own music had the effect of undistorting demand; enabling people to share that music with everyone via social media was an enhanced proposition consumer never asked for but quickly grew to love once they had it.

Many of these new propositions, linking the digital and physical worlds, exploit ubiquitous connectivity and the abundance of data. In fact, many advances in B2B business models rely on things like remote monitoring and machine-to-machine communication to create new ways of delivering value. Philips gives consumers apps as a digital enrichment of its physical-world lighting solutions. Google's Nest improves home thermostats. FedEx gives real-time insights into the progress of deliveries. In this lower-left zone, customers get entirely new value propositions that augment the ones they already had.

What are the indicators of potential disruption in this position on the matrix, as companies offer enhanced value propositions to deepen and advance their customers' expectations? You may be vulnerable if any of the following is true:

- Information or social media could greatly enrich your product or service.

- You offer a physical product, such as thermostats, that's not yet "connected."

- There's a significant lag time between the point when customers purchase your product or service and when they receive it.

- The customer must go and get the product—for instance, rental cars and groceries.

These factors indicate opportunities for improving the connectivity of physical devices, layering social media on top of products and services, and extending those products and services through digital features, digital or automated distribution approaches, and new delivery and distribution models.

131

Refocussed business systems

Delivering these new value propositions, in turn, requires rethinking, or reimagining, the business systems underlying them. Incumbents that have long focused on perfecting their industry value chains are often stunned to find new entrants introducing completely different ways to make money. Over the decades, for example, hard-drive makers have labored to develop ever more efficient ways to build and sell storage. Then Amazon (among others) came along and transformed storage from a product into a service, Dropbox upped the ante by offering free online storage, and suddenly an entire industry is on shaky ground, with its value structure in upheaval.

The forces present in this zone of the framework change how value chains work, enable step-change reductions in both fixed and variable costs and help turn products into services. These approaches often transform the scalability of cost structures—driving marginal costs toward zero and, in economic terms, flattening the supply curve and shifting it downward.

Some incumbents have kept pace effectively. Liberty Mutual developed a self-service mobile app that speeds transactions for customers while lowering its own service and support costs. The New York Times virtualized newspapers to monetize the demand curve for consumers, provide a compelling new user experience, and reduce distribution and production costs. And Walmart and Zara have digitally integrated supply chains that create cheaper but more effective operations.

Indicators of disruption in this zone include these:

- redundant value-chain activities, such as a high number of handovers or repetitive manual work

- well-entrenched physical distribution or retail networks

- overall industry margins that are higher than those of other industries

High margins invite entry by new participants, while value-chain redundancies set the stage for removing intermediaries and going directly to customers. Digital channels and virtualized services can substitute for or reshape physical and retail networks.

Hyper scaling platforms

Companies like Apple, Tencent, and Google are blurring traditional industry definitions by spanning product categories and customer segments. Owners of such hyper-scale platforms enjoy massive operating leverage from process automation, algorithms, and network effects created by the interactions. These platform owners often have goals that are distinct from those of traditional industry players.

Moreover, their operating leverage provides an opportunity to upsell and cross-sell products and services without human intervention, and that in turn provides considerable financial advantages. Amazon's objective in introducing the Kindle was primarily to sell books and Amazon Prime subscriptions, making it much more flexible in pricing than a rival like Sony, whose focus was e-reader revenues. When incumbents fail to plan for potential moves by players outside their own ecosystems, they open themselves up to the fate of camera makers, which became collateral damage in the smartphone revolution.

The hyper-scale platforms also create new barriers to entry, such as the information barrier created by GE Healthcare's platform, Centricity 360, which allows patients and third parties to collaborate in the cloud. Like Zipcar's auto-sharing service, these platforms harness first-mover and network effects. And by redefining standards, as John Deere has done with agricultural data, a platform forces the rest of an industry to integrate into a new ecosystem built around the platform itself.

What are the indicators that hyper-scale platforms, and the dynamics they create, could bring disruption to your door? Look for these situations:

- Existing business models charge customers for information.

- No single, unified, and integrated set of tools governs interactions between users and suppliers in an industry.

- The potential for network effects is high.

These factors invite platform providers to lock in users and suppliers, in part by offering free access to information.

These forces and factors come together to provide a comprehensive road-map for potential digital disruptions. Executives can use it to consider everything at once—their own business, supply chain, subindustry, and the broader industry, as well as the entire ecosystem and how it interacts with other ecosystems. They can then identify the full spectrum of opportunities and threats, both easily visible and more hidden.

Digital's impact on strategy

By starting with the supply-and-demand fundamentals, the insurance executives mentioned earlier ended up with a more profound understanding of the nature and magnitude of the digital opportunities and threats that faced them. Since they had recognized some time ago that the cross-subsidies their business depended on would erode as aggregators made prices more and more transparent, they had invested in direct, lower-cost distribution. Beyond those initial moves, the lower half of the framework had them thinking more fundamentally about how car ownership, driving, and customer expectations for insurance would evolve, as well as the types of competitors that would be relevant.

It seems natural that customers will expect to buy insurance only for the precise use and location of a car and no longer be content with just a discount for having it garaged. They'll expect a different rate depending on whether they're parking the car in a garage, in a secured parking station, or on a dimly lit street in an unsavory neighborhood. Rather than relying on crude demographics and a driver's history of accidents or offenses, companies will get instant feedback, through telematics, on the quality of driving.

In this world, which company has the best access to information about where a car is and how well it is driven, which could help underwrite insurance? Insurance companies? Car companies? Or is it consumer device makers that might know the driver's heart rate, how much sleep the driver had the previous night, and whether the driver is continually distracted by talking or texting while driving? If value accrues to superior information, car insurers will need to understand who, within and beyond the traditional insurance ecosystem, can gather and profit from the most relevant information. It's a point that can be generalized, of course. All companies, no matter what industry, will need to look for threats—and opportunities—well beyond boundaries that once seemed secure.

The digital disruption can be a frightening game, especially when some of the players are as yet out of view. By subjecting the sources of disruption to systematic analysis solidly based on the fundamentals of supply and demand, executives can better understand the threats they confront in the digital space—and search more proactively for their own opportunities.

■   ■   ■

Chapter 5: Digital Transformation Leadership

The objective of this chapter is to discuss digital leadership essentials. What are the common traits of digital leadership and how to help organizations succeed with strong leadership? This would help your organizations to prepare and transform your organization into the global Industry 4.0 standards. A lot of leaders face challenges in terms of transformation initiatives due to lack of acceptance from the stakeholders. Well, the truth is most of the stakeholders do not realize the tangible benefits of digitization unless competitors do it. By the time, they start the digital initiatives; their competitors would have created additional market opportunities. There is the misconception of digital transformation, which was conceived as digitization of paper into digital formats into processes. These digitization dimensions of turning paper into digital information are an opportunity but not necessarily business transformation in the broad sense.

For example back offices in digital banking – legacy systems and silos as digital transformation challenges. The Digital transformation projects require several elements to succeed and digitization is a part of it. Among the many elements, I'd like to focus on the core areas such as technology, people and/or processes. We have faced several challenges in terms of managing training program, communication challenges and stakeholder management etc. It's a transformation program that will need strong focus, leadership commitment, stakeholder support, scope and business operations support. Now, let us explore the key digital leadership dimensions as highlighted below in Figure 5-2 Leadership dimensions.

Digital Transformation Leadership Dimensions

In Digital transformation economy, it is imperative to possess skills to become a global leader. The four key dimensions of a Digital leadership is illustrated below in Figure 5-2

Figure 5-2 Digital Leadership Dimension

Entrepreneurship

In a digital leadership context of entrepreneurship relates to the qualities to lead the organization with increased customer focus with a mindset of creating value for all stakeholders with the attributes mentioned below:

a. Customer focus and centricity - A digital leadership should be focussed on understanding what customer wants. A digital leader would put things from a customer perspective and not just the I.T solution implementation to support customers.

b. Managerial Courage and visionary – Demonstrating courage in implementing programs to benefit customers and the organization with a vision of creating value for the business.

c. Value creation – As stated above, demonstrate value to the business by applying a continuous improvement mindset and innovativeness.

Collaboration

In a digital leadership context, collaboration relates to the influence and working together across geography. Demonstrating an ability to find synergies working together across boundaries and trusting each other with the attributes mentioned below:

- Open Communication – Communicate openly without barriers

- Transparency – Being open and transparent

- Trust – Behave in a manner that is trustful and trustworthy

Global Vision

In a digital economy, it's imperative to align with the global vision of the organization and drive strategy towards the common vision with the attributes mentioned below:

- Diversity – Embrace diversity as a key enabler

- Awareness of the Global Markets – Awareness of the global markets and its actors

- Beyond barriers in visualizing big picture – Understanding the decisions and actions taken will create a positive outcome for the benefit of the organization.

Agility

In a digital world, time quotient is reduced. It's important to be agile with the following attributes mentioned below:

- Quick Decision Making – Be responsible for quick decision making with an appropriate sense of urgency

- Embracing change – Embrace change and drive

- Bold to take initiatives – Taking initiatives by identifying opportunities and acting upon them

I'd like to remind you of the 7 Keys of success for managing a transition program successfully as illustrated below in Figure 5-1 7 Keys of success in order to manage digital transformation programs successfully as illustrated below.

DISRUPT YOUR BUSINESS before others do

The Digital Leaders will need to create their own Digital roadmap and plan for their business, which should be based on customer requirements and feedback from customers. The core outcomes should be centred around how they can provide better value proposition to their customers. The long-dominant companies are increasingly under attack from a host of digital start-ups that are able to disrupt businesses by addressing consumer needs in entirely new ways.

For example, we discussed Uber's digital strategy transforming the taxi business and Airbnb in travel. The pace of disruption is rapidly increasing in every domain. The digital disrupters are themselves constantly under attack, as witnessed by the start-ups targeting established companies such as Facebook, itself once a disrupter, Facebook share was marginalised by WhatsApp to the extent that Facebook should buy WhatsApp for a huge sum of amount.

These businesses should be more disruptive in their approach and not leave the playing field open, the advantage that Large companies hold a lot of cards— including best resources & talent pool, assets, relationships, and historic data. However, they are often do not fundamentally rethink to change their business model. Only rarely do they launch anything that might disrupt the current business entirely.

The digital CEOs must think holistically on how to innovate around the pain points of their customers. The digital transformation is not only about a website and a fabulous marketing campaign; more important, it's about entirely new business opportunities with new revenue streams.

7 Keys to Success

Figure 5-1 7 Keys of Digital Transformation

1. Stakeholders commitment to the Digital Transformation
2. Business benefits are realized
3. Risks are mitigated
4. Delivery Organization (I.T Dept.) benefits are being realized
5. Work & Schedule are predictable
6. Scope is realistic
7. Digital I.T Team is high performing

Stakeholder commitment

It is important to align with all stakeholders and gain consensus to ensure a successful transformation. Hence, the management team must provide incentives tied to digital project outcomes. Also, adequate measures required in change management and training with key subject matter experts available full-time.

A Digital leader should mitigate the following issues:

- Lack of executive sponsor focus

- People sabotaging efforts

- Resistance to new ideas

- Lack of subject matter experts availability &

- Business benefits are realized

It is important to align with all stakeholders between I.T and the business leaders with compelling reasons to implement with tangible outcomes at regular intervals. A digital initiative need not be fancy; it should be measurable outcomes based benefits to the business. Thus, business leaders will gain confidence with every release. This can be an agile-sprint type of solution, where a leader can summon accomplishments on a quarterly basis and share the vision of the digital organization.

A digital leader should watch out for the following issues:

- Why are we doing this?

- Time is not important &

- Cost is too important

Work & Schedule are predictable

A common alignment across the board is very important. A digital leader is responsible for sharing the vision, good evidence of control, with details of slippage if happens and the plan to mitigate risks.

A digital leader should watch out for the following:

- Lack of project management best practices, thus leading to a lack of planning, control, and tracking mechanisms
- Slippage comes in as a surprise

The scope is realistic and managed

A common healthy negotiation between I.T and Business teams with alignment across the board is very important. A digital leader is responsible for sharing the scope, goals to achieve in regular intervals. As a good practice to maintain issue log with agreed ways of working in terms of work allocation, assignment, and completion with more transparency

A digital leader should watch out for the following:

- Lack of team voice over issues
- Lack of documentary evidence of issues

The team is high performing

It is important to maintain good team morale, with diversified teams. As you know, we are working in a World of globalization, hence it is important to ensure all teams across the globe are aligned and work towards a common goal.

A digital leader should watch out for the following:

- Often times, the team lacks vision and feel the tension
- Turnover is high &
- Poor working conditions

Risks mitigated

It is important to align with all stakeholders to bring in more transparency in terms of risks with scoring and prioritize the critical ones with the highest impact. A good risk log with the documented plan is absolutely necessary.

Key things to watch out:

- Often people questioning, what is the risk?
- Lack of focus in mitigating risks with a process driven approach
- Delivery Organization benefits are realized

It is important to align with the business stakeholders and gain consensus to ensure the successful transformation. As discussed earlier in the initial chapters, the I.T organization must keep all stakeholders aligned about the digital transformation program strategy and benefits. A good digital leader will inspire the teams, where people feel they're learning. Second, willingness from the key stakeholders to invest in the project and finally, good articles to create awareness amongst employees.

Key points to watch out for:

- Lack of skill and availability of good staff
- Negative remarks about the performance

Change management

As it is the case in virtually all impactful changes that affect multiple stakeholders, divisions, processes and technologies (including implementing an enterprise-wide marketing ROI approach, a content marketing strategy or an integrated marketing approach with CRM, marketing automation, etc. to mention three marketing-related ones), there is not only an opportunity for change and looking at what can be done better and what should be (re)connected but also a need for change management.

If things change too fast for people or we are not taking into account the individuals that are touched, as well as their concerns, this can be a recipe for failure and at broader scale even resistance. Knowing the role of data and analytics in digital transformation, there are even more opportunities for change and needs for change management. This is not new: when web analytics became popular, for instance, their implementation and the connection between different data and analytics "silos" in the customer/marketing space often showed clear needs for digital transformation in many customer-facing and customer-oriented operations, long before the term digital transformation became known. Grasp those opportunities and tackle the challenges.

Project Measurement

The above table highlights the project scorecard. As you've observed, a good leader will be responsible for controlling each of the above parameters. As a RED color indicates high risk, leaders must take the necessary steps to avert a disaster. These are common challenges across projects, however, one of the most critical ones is the stakeholder's commitment, as we have observed digital initiatives are long-term, and hence tangible benefits are not available in the short-term. Hence, a leader is responsible for ensuring transparency in terms of discussing the return on investments (ROI) calculations and distribute it across the board. If the break-even is likely to be achieved over a period of 2/3 years, let the truth be revealed to the board to align with all stakeholders.

People and processes

As discussed in the earlier chapters, people stand first in terms of embracing digital change management first and foremost obviously is about the human dimension: internal customers, stakeholders and the broader ecosystems within which organizations reside. If things change too fast for people or we are not taking into account the individuals that are touched, as well as their concerns, this can be a recipe for failure and at broader scale even resistance.

Intent and priorities

Perhaps, you may find a lot of standard template roadmaps for digital transformation project. However, roadmaps are what they are and the intent, priorities, pain points and actual needs of the individual business and the people in its ecosystem, within a broader reality, matters more.

We do not believe in a standard template fitting all solution and intent, outcomes and priorities steer the digital transformation efforts in addition to the changing parameters in the ecosystem. Priorities also mean prioritization, often including looking at the low hanging fruit but always with the next steps and ultimate goals in mind, knowing these goals - and the context within which they were set will evolve.

Digitization Readiness

A lot of leaders believe that their organization is ready for profound digital transformation in a broad way. There may be far too many gaps in regards to the digitization and automation of existing processes and the digitization of data from legacy. Mostly, customers relate digital transformation as "just" digitization, for example, turning paper into electronic information into processes.

You'll need digitization in order to optimize in a digital transformation context. What matters is the combination, strategic and prioritized interconnecting and the actions that you take to achieve business goals through digitization and combining data.

Furthermore, there is an even bigger gap between back-office processes and the front end. An example of this phenomenon can be seen in the banking or financial industry, where there are extremely strong disconnects between the departments. There are lots and lots of digitization efforts that still need to be done in many areas of business. Perhaps a lot of administrative overheads can be cut-down eventually as a result of a transformation.

Silos, responsibility, and skills

The Digital transformation, just as a social business, digital business and any form of customer-centric marketing and business processes, requires the ability to work across silos. In many cases, digital transformation even is about totally reworking organizational structures, which can be as much about collaborative methods such as COE (Centre of Excellence) as removing specific silos.

The debate about the responsibility for digital transformation as a whole and within specific functions and processes in that sense of genuine transformation is archaic, even if it needs to be held as Chief Digital Officers, CIOs and other CxOs all play a role. Here again, there is no ideal solution regarding responsibility: context does matter.

Digital transformation and linear management thinking

With digital transformation being a de facto very hyper-connected reality on human, societal and various business and technology levels, linear management thinking and silo-based approaches make a place for hybrid, integrated, inclusive and fluid ecosystem views beyond the classic extended enterprise model.

In practice, this means that executives need to have a far better understanding and skill set regarding the various domains which are involved in digital transformation processes. A digital leader needs to understand customer-centricity. A lead will drill down into many parts of business process re-engineering, cybersecurity, IT and more. The list doesn't end there. As the drivers of technological innovations also shape the directions in which economies and businesses move the ability to connect the dots and step away from linear view towards elasticity and hybrid approaches. Understanding the impact of transformations in so many areas is probably one of the main challenges for executives.

What matters is that digital transformation takes into account all the parameters that are needed to succeed, depending on your strategy, roadmap, goals, stakeholders, context and so forth. What also matters to us is that you don't look at the digital transformation from a pure technology nor a pure marketing or any other angle.

The truth is that this gap is often exaggerated and closing. In many organizations, the gap between sales and marketing is bigger than that between the CMO and CIO or marketing and IT. Bridging these gaps is an essential part of a digital transformation strategy. Focus areas for the digital transformation leaders as highlighted below:

• Digital Technology: Enablement of digital technology to keep up the pace with your customers and ecosystems.

Partner Ecosystem: Engage strong partnerships with innovative and service-oriented leaders to facilitate a people-oriented digital transformation with clear goals and involvement of all stakeholders. In order to create great partnerships and creating a digital and social culture, the digital leader has a responsibility of learning, collaborating, understanding and empowering as well. Social and digital are a reality and so is the connected buyer's journey. A leader should accept it and look at how you can serve your customers better taking all this into account.

147

In the end, that's what the leader will do too. But you can't do it without a customer-centric.

2. Digital Marketing: Enabling integrated marketing with customer experiences but also about integrating marketing within the broader business context of other departments, connected systems, aligned processes, etc. The continuously growing marketing automation space, data and analytics, the cloud computing marketing and sales stack etc.; And let's not forget information in general as the driver of innovation, insights, interactions (what content marketing is partially about), collaboration and so much more.

The digital leader is responsible for the digital customer experience, even if some organizations have created functions such as the Chief Digital Officer (CDO). Digital transformation and integration also mean closer connections with others in the organization that have a clear role in the technological evolutions.

So, this role will be shared within and even beyond the organization with the CDO leader certainly being the partner. In fact, the CDO also will watch over the customer experience, be it in a much broader context, namely the customers as all stakeholders in the digital corporate ecosystem: employees, partners, buyers, vendors and much more. He becomes a manager of an enablement with a clear focus on IT services and – indeed – being of service, driven by business and customer goals.

It is moving to this enablement and service function. From the back-end to the front-end after having made the opposite move when ERP came around. The CDOs role is becoming one of managing the relationships with all providers and internal and external customers where IT and digital technology come into play in that famous third platform area of cloud-based, mobile-driven and data-intensive pervasive or ubiquitous technology.

• Change Management: Leading the change in terms of the – increasingly – digital, social, mobile and ubiquitous customer experience.

Summary

In this chapter, you've studied the importance of Digital transformation leadership essentials to succeed in the endeavor with the help of 7 Keys of success in managing a large and complex digital program.

A digital transformation program will need the massive scale of integrating I.T landscape with the business. This means every employee should realize the value that the program will achieve. Also, you've studied good digital leader's dos and don'ts with key watch-outs to ensure a successful digital transformation program.

■ ■ ■

Chapter 6: Benefits of Transformation

The objective of this chapter is to discuss the benefits of the Industry 4.0- Digital Transformation to the business with key risks and challenges faced during the program implementation. This would help your organizations to prepare and transform the organization into the global Industry 4.0 standards. Based on the case study that we discussed in the earlier chapters, it is important to understand the tangible benefits to the business.

Digital Business Transformation

As you know a decade ago, organizations were using digital tools and technology to help business operations. However, the primary objectives had been developing I.T solutions to support business. This approach of yesteryears resulted in consolidating the enormous amount of data on one side, and on the other side, a lot of custom applications developed over a period of time. Thus, I.T landscape became over complex without being able to provide solutions to the business. Eventually, these tools and technology became an overhead expense without supporting business in ROI. What is the use of historic data without any predictions out of it? The current state of the I.T landscape is to support the business operations, however, without I.T landscape had failed to support innovation.

Well, don't you worry! Your investments can be maximized by turning into Digital solutions. Your organization historic data can be harnessed for maximizing returns. The future strategy of Digital I.T solutions is to support business with innovation. Therefore, running I.T solutions will be simplified with data readily available for the business. With innovative solutions supporting business to continuously improve and expand market capabilities, while I.T systems can harness the true potential of data and market survey, customer preferences by using analytic information.

Thus, by leveraging digital solutions, your systems will become lean. The I.T operational expenses are reduced, taking out a major chunk of your operational issues, helping your business to focus more on strategy, rather than fixing problems. With the increased number of users, cloud services, and connected devices, businesses are using digital technology to develop deeper engagement with the business operations. By transforming an organization to digital, you can take advantage of emerging opportunities, establishing a company culture that encourages creativity and innovation.

The Digital Transformation - Industry 4.0 is the upcoming standard. It denotes Smart Industry or the Industrial Internet with tangible benefits for manufacturers to transform the way they work. The essential goal of Industry 4.0 is to make industries smart by using smarter solutions, which are efficient and customer-centric. The main objective is to go beyond automation to expand into newer markets and evolve into an innovative business model. For example, OLA is a classic example. They had created a newer revenue stream for customers, employees. The tangible benefits our customers can use the options and save money, time with safety using IoT solutions that keep track of the taxi.

The key benefits of transforming Industry 4.0 are to improve efficiency and productivity with the usage of the digital technologies such as the Internet of Things (IoT), robots in manufacturing and it supports operations to support innovation in every department. To summarize the core benefits as highlighted below:

1.   Improve Efficiency

2.   Enhance Customer value & reach

3.   Empower your employees

4.   Improved decision making

5.   Improved profitability & competitiveness &

6.   Overall improved productivity

Improve Efficiency

If you want to improve the overall efficiency of the business operations, it is important to provide the necessary tools to the users, where key users can collaborate and share information easily. For instance, with the right digital tools, teams can easily collaborate between departments and locations, making business decisions and operations more streamlined. Thus, by effectively collaborating, ideas flow from the business to the I.T and various departments to improve ways of working, solve problems and meet deadlines. Overall, the impact of this collaboration would be increased productivity and customer care. The arrival of unified messaging and communication tools such as Office 365 and Skype, WhatsApp. Each of the unified communication tools can be used to communicate, collaborate to solve business problems as one team across the globe.

Enhance Customer Value & reach

As we discussed in earlier chapters with various case studies, the core area of improvement is to help customers feel happy. Indeed, this is possible by only providing simple tools that can help customers' achieve what they want. These experiences of a customer will help you retain them and grow. The digital experience is far more superior in providing a competitive edge. Say, for example, Amazon.in is a great platform for customers, whose buying preferences are studied by the tool suite. Therefore, it is easy to understand what a customer wants finally. Every click on products and services is tracked by the tool suite to propagate intelligent messages based on the historical evidence of the customer's buying pattern. By investing more in digital technologies such as AI/Big data, it is possible to build new products and services to retain the current customers, as well as wing over new ones.

The ultimate benefit is the Customer satisfaction, loyalty and retention have always been important for business survival and growth. A strong customer experience means stronger customer loyalty, more sales, and more new customers through referrals. Your business must spend time identifying how to interact with customers at the right time, in the right place. The first step in transformation is to identify tools that can help your customers. Once you understand your customers' journey and behaviors, you'll be in a strong position to create a digital plan accordingly and begin the process of choosing the right technology you need to carry it out to its fullest. Most of these CRM packages such as SAP CRM, Oracle focus on lead generation and supporting artifacts of discussions. One of the best tools in the market available in salesforce.com, which has captured the market globally through innovative products and solutions for closer interaction with customers;

You can access information about your customers online using customer relationship management tools – where you can collect contact information, business website behavior, and customer purchase and service behavior – can significantly enhance your consumer engagement strategy.

For instance, Amazon.com and flipkart.com are great examples of a successful e-commerce platform for buyers and sellers. These platforms provide users with variable buying options, preferences etc. The sellers can get insights into the customer preferences with detailed sales analysis.

In the current scenario, customers are reaching out to businesses via so many different channels. Now, the key question for all organization unanimously is to identify ways to offer enhanced customer experience. It takes good customer data to deliver great service. The right digital tool can help you save time and run your business efficiently whilst you leverage business data to stay ahead of the competition. Improved customer satisfaction – In the current situation, customers expect to have what they want, when they want it, with a supreme value from any device in real time with increased transparency. However, the technology used need be disclosed to the customers. It has to simple solutions for complex business problems. Indeed, we are discussing a robust technology platform that can offer benefits to the customer. With the rise of mobile and technology advancements, we've observed changing customer behavior. The modern customer wants simplicity. What happens if you can't provide the simplicity they expect? What happens if you make them jump through the legacy and outdated applications? If a customer takes longer to identify products in the organization's portal or order a service, perhaps there is a chance that opportunity is lost for you.

By investing in a digital transformation, customers will appreciate that you are focused on their needs and experience. By transforming for the digital age, companies are transforming in to valuing customer's time with quick turn-around in products and services and make life easier for the clientele. This would in-turn help companies to prosper with more happy customers.

Improve reach

We discussed the digital efforts, which will help companies. I explained how mobile makes 24/7 even longer with application integration via m-commerce platform. In short, it puts your product or service at your potential customer's fingertips at any time. Just think about it, What if your customers/prospects could learn about your business and make a purchase at any time, and from anywhere? Or, on the other hand, what if they wanted to make a purchase…but your company had no mobile presence?

For instance, I like shopping at Amazon.in, wherein you have a choice of buying a paperback book or digital copy or audiobook in the format that you like. A similar approach for movies, perhaps you can download content, procure a cd or whatever format you like. A digital transformation should put everything in front of the customers. They should enable more transparency in terms of products, services and open to discussing price options. This transformation process involves making your business available to your customers/prospects, from anywhere. When your business website and applications adapt to any device, you're in front of your prospects and customers all the time.

The current trend in digital transformation is about enabling anytime, anywhere transacting. For instance, digital banking is a classic example. It has changed the banking industry completely. As a consumer, I have a choice to do mobile banking for almost everything. A decade ago, I started using online banking, instead of waiting in the queue for cheque deposits or withdrawals. Now, I am using m-banking for almost every transaction such as transfers, investments etc. Perhaps, the future would transform into a global digital wallet, instead of wastage in printing currency. I can utilize the wait time into productive time. This is exactly the goal of every company so it can minimize drop off during a transaction, meet customer expectations and deliver exceptional service on any device.

Empower Your Employees

It's good to be customer-centric, however, if your in-house employees are not happy, nothing can happen in the customer front. If your employees are happy, they will keep customers happy. Therefore, it is important to ensure empowering employees and partners to ensure a successful transformation journey. The first step is to start by providing the necessary tools such as unified communication tools to improve productivity. With appropriate skill training, coaching and succession plan as part of the HR activities, you can transform into the digital organization. Giving your employees with necessary tools and training will enable them to be more proficient at their jobs, resulting in greater employee empowerment. For example, your staff will not only be able to instantaneously collaborate with colleagues and management but also consult with experts and get questions answered in real time. The rapid globalization has necessitated employees to work from virtually anywhere, anytime, allowing your team to fully optimize their time.

Improved decision making

You might have observed a data explosion in the past few years. As a business, you have access to more data than ever before, and data volumes are only increasing. However, very few businesses actually capitalize on this data. With proper digital big data tools, you can leverage information to the fullest to service your customer requirements. Using modern analytic tools, you'll gain insights immediately. This would help customers to do things faster and innovative.

In the current scenario, cutting-edge software tools feed off digital data with better decision making in essential functions like ad spend optimization, sales lead prioritization, customer communications, and even employee performance. Furthermore, digital tools such as AI/Bi data will help you in harnessing data by providing insights. FOR instances, 10 years of historical data can be evidence of your corporate performance across departments. You can finalize the areas of improvement based on the historical data. Also, real-time changes are possible by investing in AI tools to support on-the-fly decision making using data and AI algorithm almost real-time. For instance, you can optimize plant operations by leveraging the past history. You can plan your plant's maintenance activities. There is the lot more that you bring it on to the table. Thanks to social media, mobile, credit cards, and ubiquitous online

155

connectivity, there is an abundance of information to help companies improve their processes.

Improved Profitability & Competitiveness

What happens when you more efficiently, make better decisions and improve customer's perception of your business? How will that impact your bottom line? The fact is that digital transformation will transform your entire business.

As explained below, when done correctly, it will significantly improve your overall profitability. These companies that intensely embrace digital within their systems and business models can significantly increase revenue and company valuation, but those who do so without effective change management will risk profitability. These Digital transformation projects that drive digital initiatives with the real commitment to all-encompassing change management will reach even greater improvements in profitability.

The bottom line is that technology is transforming the business world. There is no question that digital transformation is no longer a choice. To stay competitive and survive, build a business that can adapt its technology and strategies rapidly.

Enhanced productivity through automation

It's easy to comprehend productivity improvements through automation. However, the key question is transformation and not automating in the silo. The blueprint of the entire end-to-end operations should be studied to finalize the transformation plan. As mentioned in the earlier section optimization of processes lead to productivity improvements. It's also one of the first goals of Industry 4.0 projects. There are a lot of opportunities to save costs, increasing profitability, reducing waste and automation to reduce defects etc. Digital transformation helps in improving the overall value chain, where speed is crucial for everyone, digitizing paper-based flows, being able to intervene faster in case of production defects.

The Internet of Things (IoT) solutions helps in manufacturing operations from optimized asset utilization and smoother production processes to better logistics and inventory management. The real-time data for a real-time supply chain in a real-time economy. While we just mentioned speed in a context of optimization, automation, and enhanced productivity, it is a benefit in many other ways as well. The main benefits of digitization are to improve productivity, enhance customer centricity. The Industry 4.0 standards encompass the entire life cycle of products design to supply chain, manufacturing, quality, and services will need to realize benefits of the Industry 4.0.

If you look at the entire value chain and ecosystem within which manufacturing operations reside there are many stakeholders involved. These are all customers. As you realize, customers want enhanced productivity, regardless of where they sit in the supply chain. Moreover, there are factors such as on-time delivery (OTD) with desired quality with six sigma standards with better customer experiences.

The Industry 4.0 transformation involves smart factories, supply chains, informed customers, and alignment: it's all about data, from the actual operations to the delivery of a product to an end customer and beyond. The more data you gather early on and the more time this data gets where it matters when it matters, the more value down the supply chain.

Digital Tech & Data protection

Every organization is turning to cloud solutions for critical business applications, data storage, and backup. The Cloud solutions are hosted and managed in monitored and controlled facilities, designed to minimize downtime and keep data well protected.

Create a Data Security Policy

In the world of digital transformation, Data security and privacy policies are very important to keep data safe. A large customer care center implemented policies to protect customer's sensitive data. You might have observed several instances of lost or stolen data. Hence, it is imperative for every organization to ensure policies for data transfer and security protocols. For example, in today's digital organization, there are so many channels accessing your organization's information. Hence, policies should be very specific in terms of acceptable and not acceptable to employees and customers. These policies should indicate e-mails policies, mobile access, and social media guidelines. These policies should be well documented, communicated, enforced and periodically reviewed and updated. Usually, the Data Security & Privacy (DS&P) team is responsible for policy reviews and communication. The DS&P team will be taking care of training program and creating awareness amongst employees.

Physical and Cybersecurity Controls

All basic physical security access controls must be done first as a top priority to avoid non-compliance. For example, access to office buildings with necessary physical security controls and cyber security controls leveraged by the service provider. Physical security controls such as badge access to get into the building? Or even better, a biometric? Furthermore, from data access and security perspective it is important to lay down cybersecurity protocols. For example, firewall protection, network monitoring, and wireless security? It is important to encrypt data. It's important to ensure partners are communicated about the protocols and understand the service level agreements (SLA's) for system availability. In addition, you should understand their policy around data breaches. How do your partners rectify incidents?

Enhanced Business continuity

As a leader, you may have encountered several production downtimes and disruption for various reasons. One of the key challenges for any leader is to ensure smooth operations without much disruption. Your production lines must continue without issues. If for some reason, any asset break-down in the production facility, then it will lead to loss of money, valuable efforts put it by many engineers to resolve the incident occurred. For example, when a key asset such as industrial robot breaks-down in a car manufacturing plant, then the production line will be severely affected. This would increase the costs, delivery schedule leading to unhappy customers. The production downtime due to an incident is always a nightmare to everyone.

Now, the question is how to avoid such incidents? This is where the Industry 4.0 transformation will help through IoT implementation connected to your back office. This infrastructure will help you close monitoring of the plant and help you plan scheduled maintenance or before an incident occurs. The alerts sent by IoT can be proactively maintained, real-time monitoring and diagnosis become possible, engineers can fix issues if they do occur from a distance, and the list goes on. Moreover, patterns and insights are gained to optimize in areas where things seem to have issued more often and a world of new maintenance services. No wonder that asset management and maintenance are the second largest area of IoT investments in manufacturing.

Through real-time monitoring, IoT-enabled quality improvement, quality of the product is managed well. In a digital economy customers' demand OTD (on-time delivery). However, that doesn't mean they are ready trade-off quality for speed. If you have everything in your production system and its broader environment connected with sensors, software, IoT technologies, and AI systems of insight to support a digital enterprise to deliver a high-quality product. Usage of cyber-physical systems and the Internet of Things helps you in monitoring quality of products real-time to avert a disaster.

Industry 4.0 challenges and risks

Let's observe key risks and challenges as highlighted below:

- Establishing a common strategy, goals, and vision of Industry 4.0 across the board

- Defining an outcome-based model. This would involve a rethinking of the organization and processes to maximize outcomes.

- Understanding the business case.

- Conducting successful pilots.

- Making the organization realize action is needed.

- Change management is very important

- Transforming to Innovative culture.

- A true interconnection of departments &

- Talent Management for Digital skills

There are many other challenges observed as highlighted below:

1.   I.T Systems: Transforming legacy information systems to a centralized Information management excellence. It is not required to complete replacements, it can be extensions to be able to access data readily and harness for business benefits. It's all about actionable intelligence and connected information and process excellence in a context of relevance, innovation and timely availability for any desired business, employee and obviously customer goal.

2.   Cybersecurity and privacy: We discussed data security and privacy. It's important to establish protocols to protect data. The increasing number of attacks in the Industrial Internet of Things is fact as IT and OT converge is a key component of Industry 4.0.

On top of these challenges there are several others, practical, technological and ecosystem-related:

- The challenges regarding the integration of IT and Operational Technology (OT).

- Data compliance questions.

- Managing risk and lowering costs in uncertain times.

- Dealing with the complexity of the connected supply chain.

- A better understanding of IT and OT technologies and, more importantly, how they can be leveraged.

- Altering customer and industrial partner demands.

- Competition and the fact that Industry 4.0 champions gain a competitive benefit fast.

- The eternal and extremely important human challenge (talent, future of work, employment,).

The above-mentioned challenges exist today, as some of you have observed in the ongoing programs, while others will need to step up their pace. It's the right time to sprint to value in Industry 4.0 in a world where digital transformation is a marathon with several sprints.

Better working conditions and sustainability

It's important to provide good working conditions in order to motivate and keep employees healthy. Indeed, if we consider improving condition of the employees at the plant such as better environment, humidity then the productivity of employees will increase drastically. Moreover, if we look at the possibilities and benefits, that human, social and even environmental aspect in Industry 4.0

For example, improving working conditions based on real-time temperature, humidity and other data in the plant or warehouse, quick detection and enhanced protection in case of incidents, detection of presence of gasses, radiation and so forth, better communication and collaboration possibilities, a focus on ergonomics, clean air and clean factory initiatives (certainly in Industry 4.0 as the EU wants to be leading in clean air and clean anything technologies), the list goes on.

Personalization for the digital consumer

It's important to understand consumer behavior and preferences. These Digital tools have changed the ways we work, shop and live. Mostly, customers have become more demanding with regards to fast responses and timely information/deliveries. On top of that consumers also like a degree of personalization, depending on the context. For instance, pizza toppings or ice cream toppings have increased with multiple options to choose from. This is the same in every industry. Another example is customizing preferences for cars, with the ability to customize in whatever way possible.

There is another important aspect of customer behavior that I'd like to highlight. There is an increasing trend of consumers wanting to directly interact with the brand and manufacturing capability. Therefore, Digital platforms allow customers to customize products as mentioned, shortened routes between production and delivery, possibilities to co-create and so on. In many manufacturing environments, these things already happening and it's not just in a consumer environment. We increasingly see customization in a B2B context as well, even if it's just to stick a label, add a custom feature or adapt any characteristic of the product whatsoever. For example, banks have transformed its credit card options with branding options that consumer can choose from.

Improved Agility

How can you help business to take quick decision and agile? If you'd like to be competitive in the business landscape, then you'll be able to adapt to the newer challenges. In addition to improving productivity, scalability and agility is a core part of digital transformation by using technology drivers. These drivers such as cloud, Software-as-a-Service offerings, Big Data/Analytics and AI-based services can be used for supporting business operations to be agiler. Especially in the manufacturing and its support organizations, AI can IoT services will help you with several benefits.

For example, in the manufacturing sector, Big Data, AI, robots and cyber-physical systems can help you predict and meet seasonal demand, fluctuations in production. More so with innovative capabilities that will help you build in new revenue models using digital economy. You can transform processes, specific functions, customer service, experiences, and skillsets but in the end, the true value is generated by tapping into new, often information-intensive, revenue sources and ecosystems, enabling innovative capabilities, for instance in deploying an as-a-service-capacity for customers, advanced maintenance services and so on.

Summary

While the list of benefits could certainly be longer, these are just a few examples of tangible benefits to your organization due to digital transformation. The world is changing to the digital form of evolution and it's just the beginning. The scope of transformation will transform to the next generation platform, technologies to support business operations. The fundamentals of business practices will evolve to increasing customer satisfaction, reach out to the new markets and rapid globalization. Indeed, companies will work seamlessly as one-unit with global manufacturing units in different locations; with disparate I.T systems will work as an integrated platform to support business needs. The melting point of success is where the transformation strategy helps the business to drive innovation and improve bottom-line profitability. The future of smart digital companies would evolve to the next level to engage customers, partners, and suppliers more intimately. Also, we discussed a few challenges that we will need to overcome in the pursuit of excellence.

■   ■   ■

Chapter 7: Digital Transformation Case studies

The objective of this chapter is to discuss case studies overview of the Industry 4.0- Digital Transformation. Every case study is a lesson learned by the hard experiences, this chapter will encompass critical success factors of implementation with a high-level overview. From legacy infrastructure to the state of the art digitized factories yielding year-on-year benefits to the business. These lessons learned would help your organizations to prepare and transform your organization into the global Industry 4.0 standards.

We have many examples of case studies in every sector, while some of them are still in progress, most of them have transformed into smart Industry 4.0. Now, let us understand case studies that have successfully transformed a business into the agile digital world. Perhaps, you may need to re-work on strategy, development of new competencies, agile, people-oriented, customer-centric, innovative and able to leverage opportunities to change the status quo and top service is driven revenues. Now, let us explore critical success factors in the case studies discussed at a high level in the following sectors below:

1.   Manufacturing,

a.   Logistics (Supply Chain & Transportation)

2.   Public Sector,

3.   Utilities,

4.   Insurance,

5.   Healthcare,

6.   Retail Banking

a.   Regional Banking &

7.   Business Process Outsourcing (BPO)

Digital transformation in Manufacturing

The Digital transformation of manufacturing is progressing at different speeds with the integration/convergence of Information Technology (OT) and Operational Technology (OT) as key to improve efficiency and speed.

Gone are the days of the production process using manual methods. Today, the manufacturing industry is transforming from mass production to customization. It is important to deliver high-quality products on-time with high quality at a right price. Further, customers are expecting increased transparency in the process of how products are designed and delivered at a new level of sophistication. The first step in digitization is to analyze the current state of all systems, from R&D, design, procurement, production, warehousing, logistics, and marketing to sales and service.

The digitization of manufacturing impacts every aspect of operations and the supply chain. It starts with equipment design and continues through product design, production process improvement, and ultimately, monitoring and improving the end user experience. Digital transformation revolutionizes the way manufacturers share and manage product and engineering design specs on the cloud by collaborating across geographies.

A large jet engine manufacturer combined cloud-based services, analytics, and online sensors to report usage and status and help predict potential failures. The result is improved uptime and lower cost of ownership as part of services.

The Additive manufacturing (3D printers) is used for prototyping to reduce the number of iteration cycles in the design process. This helps in continuous improvement in value. 3D printing is also quickly gaining ground in the low-volume commercial manufacturing of customized products. IoT sensors are further connecting devices to the back office in the digitally transformed smart factories. For example, Smart machines integrated with forklifts, storage shelves, and production equipment can take autonomous decisions and communicate with each other to drive material replenishment, trigger manufacturing. The Industry 4.0

allows manufacturers to have more flexible manufacturing processes that can better react to customer demands.

As you all know about the benefits of digital transformation, the key outcomes that leaders anticipate are the following:

- Optimize operations,

- Enhance customer-centricity,

- Innovate,

- Increase revenues &

- Identify new revenue streams with new business models.

The enterprise-wide digital transformation in manufacturing is compensated by the industry's leading place in one key transformative aspect of the Industry 4.0 cyber-physical, data-intensive and innovative services systems and technologies stack: the Industrial Internet of Things. Two other important notions in the digital transformation of manufacturing: digital twins and the mentioned cyber-physical systems approach. The manufacturing industry by far leads in the Internet of Things space and more and more companies leverage the huge opportunities as a result.

Transforming supply chain

There aren't many industries with as many interconnected organizations, ecosystems, processes, information flows, devices from the individual goods, boxes and pallets to trucks and ships and physical distribution and handling operations as transportation and logistics. In a context of globalization, changing customer expectations, huge pressures on margins, and high risks of enormous volumes of data, the logistics, and transportation industry is in full flux.

Strictly speaking we, of course, need to differ between the transportation of people and goods. While the transportation of people, of course, is being transformed, a large majority of digital transformation budgets goes to supply chain transformation projects with the move from the hybrid model to a full digital supply chain in mind.

In the context of the transportation of goods and the supply chain, speed, visibility, digitization and digital transformation rank high on the agenda. Given the long-standing usage of sensors and RFID, as well as the need to dispose over data which enable new business models and better processes, the (goods) transportation and logistics industry take a leading place in the deployment of Internet of Things projects, Internet of Things spending and the Industrial Internet of Things market.

Also, data analytics are big in this industry that has been used to work with big data before the term existed. However, among the many transformational challenges is the fact that data maturity levels need to go up and that digital strategies need to be deployed across end-to-end supply chains. It's a complex given in a highly complex and interconnected industry with many different activities.

Digital transformation in the public sector

The role and structure of national and local governments, government agencies, state-sponsored organizations and public sector institutions differs from country to country. However, regardless of the ways typical areas where governments are involved such as public healthcare, transport, public infrastructure, policing and defense, citizen services or regulation, are organized, there are many commonalities in the challenges and priorities, not in the least from the digital transformation perspective.

While from the citizen experience perspective the role of digital transformation becomes clear in areas such as e-government and digital identity programs, in many other areas transparency, efficiency and coordination are key in the digitization of processes and project management. Recent research shows that a majority of public sector professionals recognize the disruptive impact of digital technologies on government.

• The first driver of digital transformation in government and the public sector is cost savings in a world where populations are aging and a mix of local, national and geopolitical shifts necessitate choices and changes, whereby higher cost transparency and cost reductions are key.

• The second driver of digital transformation in government is meeting the demands of a 'digital' citizen and enhancing the citizen experience. Citizen demands are evolving because the demands of people are evolving, whether it's in their capacities as workers, consumers or citizens. Improving the citizen experience of an increasingly digital and mobile first citizen whose digital lifestyle doesn't match with the often paperwork-intensive reality that is still too dominant and causes frustration is a priority.

Digital transformation in the utility industry

Utility firms face tremendous challenges. Yet, they are at the same time active in an industry where digital transformation can lead to tremendous cost savings, new offerings, alternative pricing models, customer experience optimization and even radical new ways of 'doing business', engaging with customers and their very business model.

From a technological viewpoint, the Internet of Things, Big Data and everything related to 'smart' plays a key role. Furthermore, investments and innovations in making customers aware of their consumption and allowing them to control it in unseen ways add to the many possibilities in areas such as ecology/environment and changing supply chains.

Digital transformation in the insurance industry

The insurance industry has numerous opportunities to leverage technologies in transformational ways. Among the typical areas which are often mentioned are telematics, the Internet of Things, the use of predictive analysis (risk) and new business models and pay-as-you-go insurance approaches.

A majority of consumers would, for instance, be willing to have a sensor attached to their car or home if this would result in a reduction in premiums. Yet, just as much as technologies offer tremendous opportunities which are increasingly being embraced by insurers, there are also challenges. The changed expectations of policyholders and younger consumers play a significant role here. Moreover, there is a lot of work in an essential business process such as insurance claims management, customer service, and meet changing regulations. On top of that, there is the rise of Insurance Technology and the fact that consumers buy insurances from non-traditional providers, including retailers.

The challenges and opportunities are vast as you can read on our page about digitization and digital transformation in the insurance industry.

Digital transformation in healthcare

The digital transformation of healthcare among others is driven by the aging/growing population challenge, the rise of chronic diseases, increasing costs and the changed expectations and behavior of people.

These changing expectations and behavioral patterns obviously also impact us as patients, one of many reasons why there is an increased focus on patient-centricity. However, let's certainly also not forget healthcare workers who display changing behavior as well and use digital and mobile platforms too, which leads to an even more information-driven healthcare.

The enterprise mobile platform has totally changed the face of healthcare whereby increasing productivity and employee satisfaction is another challenge. Doctors, specialists, and nurses often have to work in increasingly difficult circumstances amidst budget cuts.

That brings us to the need for efficiency and fast access to healthcare information for all the obvious benefits. Another challenge concerns the funding of healthcare and, hence, also the leverage of digital technologies to not just save costs but also grows revenues. In some countries healthcare tourism, for example, is even a national priority as they evolve towards a more service-oriented economy.

As we move towards a more connected healthcare the Internet of Things becomes a key game changer to tackle many of the mentioned challenges and reinventions of healthcare models.

There are certainly more challenges – and opportunities – for the digital transformation of healthcare and we dive deeper into several ones on our page on digital transformation in healthcare where we also look at forecasts until 2020 and, among others, see an increase of robots who take care of easy tasks in hospitals, the growing role of remote health monitoring and new healthcare models, linked with data on our lifestyle. And of course, there is a key role for information and quite some work in the space of the digitization of health records (EHR/EMR).

Digital transformation in retail banking

Although there are several changes, disruptions and digital transformation (challenges) in retail banking some are restricted (or more/less important) to specific geographies given, for instance regulatory, consumer-related, focus-related and even broader societal elements. More about these geographical differences in "Retail banking: the growing importance of direct and digital channels".

Retail banks are increasingly collaborating with Finance Technology as they don't dispose of the speed, technology, agility, technological (non-legacy) experience and sometimes even customer experience. In some regions, these collaborative efforts are more important than in others but we clearly see a convergence of technology and incumbents in many forms and shapes.

These evolutions, as well as the many challenges, opportunities, and transformations retail banks, face on our overview page.

Digital transformation in regional banks

Of course, digital transformation is not just for retail banks, let alone for large banks. A nice digital banking framework for regional banks and community banks in practice, with a focus on mobile banking and the gradual deployment of an Omnichannel banking platform as depicted above, leveraging tools such as mobile, chatbots, digital payments and Fintech technologies used in a community banking context, although it shows deployment stages that might be relevant for larger banks too.

Digital transformation and business process outsourcing

There is a thin line between digital transformation and business process management, more specifically business process optimization and re-engineering for a digital age and customer. However, digital transformation also has a profound impact on business process outsourcing (BPO) and thus the industry of BPOs. Business process outsourcing is moving from its traditional predominant cost-saving and (outsourced) process optimization roots to a cost-plus optimization plus innovation plus value proposition.

Organizations have to change expectations from their BPO partners, who need to transform themselves, in order to meet these changing demands of disrupted customers. The Business process outsourcers need to be far more aligned with business, acquire new skills, transform and optimize their own operations, and last but not least, seek how to add more value to their propositions. When organizations transform, then so do their partners to whom they outsource specific business processes.

Key human differentiator

To understand digital transformation, it's key to put people and processes above technology, even if a technology is a change agent – or at least the ways we use it to evolve, innovate, adapt and "pro-adapt".

Digital transformation is about using digital technologies to improve (and connect and often radically change) processes, enhance customer experiences, focus on the area where business and customer value meet and seeing new and better possibilities while using different and digital-intensive ways to realize them. Digital transformation even goes beyond the use of digital technologies to support or improve processes and existing methods. It is a way to alter and even build new business models, using digital technologies. In that sense, it also goes beyond digitization (although that's often a condition to make it happen) and certainly beyond a digital-savvy skillset and capacity which is nothing less than a must in the age of an increasingly channel-agnostic and digital customer.

171

However, this so-called digital culture is not the start or essence of digital transformation. Digital transformation is also about responding to the changes that digital technologies have caused – and will continue to cause – in our daily lives, individual businesses and organizations, industries and various segments of society. These changes are obviously not brought upon us by the technologies themselves. The human dimension is not just an important focus of digital transformation, it's a catalyst whereby the ways we use and see digital technologies can have very unexpected consequences, regardless of whether it concerns consumer/customer behaviour or the innovative capacity of disruptive companies (nearly always a mix), in the end also people.

In the end, the mindset, let alone somewhat vague term 'culture', and approach we need is one of continuous optimization, holistic improvement and a focus on what people need, far beyond the digital context.

Summary

In this chapter, you've studied the benefits of Industry 4.0 – Digital Transformation with critical success factors in real-life case studies across various sectors.

It is no longer an option to migrate to Industry 4.0 to survive in the market. As you have observed across various sectors, the benefits are multi-fold. If you're contemplating about increasing revenue stream, creating additional revenues in the newer markets and want to stay ahead of the competition, then the digital transformation is clearly the way that can help you achieve these benefits.

■   ■   ■

Chapter 8: Adapting your board to the Digital age

The objective of this chapter is to discuss how to adapt b the digital age. It's an uphill task to get all stakeholders aligned with the digital transformation strategy. Now, let's understand how to make your board aligned with the future vision with customer centricity. The mindset will need to change to digital across the board to survive in the market.

The digital technologies have profoundly changed the ways we do business, buy, work and live. They have even altered society and continue impacting virtually all business functions and industries. It's partially what digital business is about.

Today, digital business mainly is used in a context of digital transformation, disruptive technologies, holistic business optimization and integration/convergence. However, it's much more than that. It's also about digital marketing transformation, social business and – as we can never forget the human element that risks being ignored amidst the avalanche of new technologies and the digital fascination – humanization. A key part of it all is information – put at work, which requires a holistic information management approach – and connecting value to create more value, throughout the entire ecosystem.

Digital information

Providing the right (access to the right) content at the right time through the right channels etc. , shaping relevant experiences, plays a key role in all customer-facing – and other – evolutions: social business, social media marketing, content marketing, integrated marketing, marketing automation, closed-loop marketing, you name it. It's just one part of what digital business is about. But information is crucial in many digital business areas, outside marketing, and customer-facing functions too. It's essential.

Digital definitions and context

As digital technologies offer new ways to connect, collaborate, conduct business and build bridges between people, it touches the core of all business functions and even the ways organizations are managed.

Digital technologies have also challenged existing business models and continue to do so. One of the key driving forces of it is the capacity of innovation and the consumerization of IT certainly also plays a role. Digital business is about that stage you see in many maturity models (in marketing, ICT, social, business, you name it): the converged – or fully connected/integrated stage. From a sheer technology perspective it goes beyond the famous third platform and the evolutions we are witnessing today: cloud computing, the Internet of Things, mobile, Big Data, etc.

Defining digital business and six steps

As mobile, social, cloud, and big data come together we see the emergence of digital business strategy: the ability to leverage digital technologies to transform the customer value equation and drive competitive advantage".

And that's where we're getting closer to Gartner's definition of digital business and see this convergence between business and IT, discussions about the role of the CIO, CMO and even CEO, the call for new job functions such as the Chief Digital Officer, etc.

The digital business is the creation of new business designs by blurring the digital and physical worlds. Sounds vague? Just look at the retail banking industry where digital technologies are increasingly used across several business functions and also in the physical branch, indeed blurring those lines.

Thus, the digital business promises to a user in an unprecedented convergence of people, business, and things that disrupts existing business models. But the people dimension needs it to be more than just about that: connecting technologies, people, information and processes with the aim to enable better customer experiences. Gartner also caused quite a stir when predicting that digital business incompetence will cause 25% of businesses to lose competitive ranking by 2017.

In May 2014, Gartner also introduced "Six Key Steps to Build a Successful Digital Business", showing the different elements. You can read more about it here and check out a graphical representation of the six steps as illustrated below. Notice the role of information as an asset and of content.

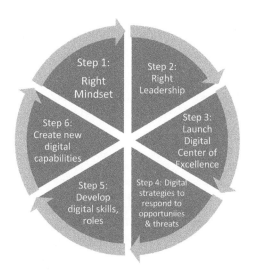

Six key steps to build a successful digital business according to Gartner – based on Gartner press release

While most digital evolutions are looked upon from a technology- and company-centric perspective, often leading to disconnected business strategies, it's important to cut through the noise and buzzwords of the day, put them in context and focus on the real questions: how to improve your efficiency, business and the lives of the people in the ecosystem you operate in.

Digital business goes beyond social business and certainly beyond marketing. It's about business and people, or as said: about experiences. And those experiences are shaped, among others, by having the proper information, resources, tools and much more, to allow choice and a partial/gradual shift of control. The "I" of IT (information) plays a key role in it, as does the context within which it resides.

The real reason why integrated marketing is important, for instance, is not (just) because it enables marketers to have a unified customer view. It's because customers don't want to be treated differently, depending on why, how and where they interact with your business. They don't want to see the organizational silos and disconnected systems, leading to poor customer experiences. They want the right information at the right time etc. The same is happening in IT, for instance, where we see customer experiences (with the customer being also employees, for instance) pop up as a parameter for success (also in enterprise applications). It's about measuring value through what you do is valued.

Digital business is also about people and processes. Because a connected digital business approach, across all functions, and a connected interaction with the ecosystem of your business can only happen if they are connecting the value dots and docs well, regardless of job function. And sometimes can disconnect. That mix is the challenge we all face in an age of digital business.

The balance between technology, efficiency, and humanity

Digital business is not just about technology, disruption or even business in the strict sense. Technology is not a holy grail. What matters is how digital technologies impact business in real life because they impact the behavior and attitudes of people across all their activities. Just consider how organizations, executives, teams and people use them to improve the ways they serve their customers, collaborate and operate.

Digital business is business with a people-centric view and agile processes, whereby digital technology is used to enable people (customers, employees, managers, etc.) to succeed, optimize all business functions and make your business more relevant and profitable. Value. It does this in the increasingly connected ecosystem in which organizations and people live and work. The CIO, CMO will need to learn from each other and not understanding the role of digital and how it is used by customer, employees and other stakeholders is not an option for any C-level exec anymore. You can't "manage" a business or business function without missing competitive benefits if you don't understand the digital reality and its' impact on customer experiences in the broadest sense.

People-centricity and humanization sometimes mean disconnecting from efficiency and technology as well. We can optimize and improve everything. Efficiency, productivity, profit, customer experiences, the ways we work and collaborate, but in the end, nothing works when we ignore that human element. We are not robots; we cannot always focus on being more productive, collaborative and connected. We need the conditions, space, and environment in which our freedom and creativity can be nurtured and cultivated. We cannot do business if we cannot be "human" and inefficient at the time.

The best way to understand the impact and role of digital technologies in today's business is by looking at it from a geographical, vertical, functional and even individual (business and customer) perspective. Each business is different, as each customer, industry, and country is different. We regularly look at digital business and digital transformation from those perspectives. An example: digital transformations and challenges in the retail banking industry - check it out here.

Now, let's understand briefly on preparing your board for the digital transformation.

Preparing board to the digital age

The change is around the corner and in today's competitive market, it is important to embrace changes to survive, even before it enforces by the way of the market. The consumers are looking at the change, whereas suppliers are changing their ways-of-working by embracing the digital era. There is only one option to survive in the upcoming market, either to change and survive or let the new entrants compete against your company and make quick wins in the market. The customers would like to see the company that is aggressive in the pursuit of change to digital. Even if it is a new entrant, consumers are willing to testify to products and services. If you're a large-cap or a mid-cap, beware that many small players have emerged as victorious entrants by venturing into digital space. Hence, it's a competitive landscape. It's not customer satisfaction alone; it's going to enhanced customer digital experience.

Therefore, most companies are feeling outmatched by the ferocity of changing technology, emerging risks, and new competitors. Here are four ways to get boards in the game. Today's boards are getting the message to go digital as fast as possible. They have seen how leading digital players are threatening incumbents, and among the directors we work with, roughly one in three say that their business model will be disrupted in the next five years.

In our experience, common responses from boards to the shifting environment include hiring a digital director or chief digital officer, making pilgrimages to Silicon Valley, and launching sub-committees on digital. These are valuable as such moves can be, they often are insufficient to bridge the literacy gap facing boards—which has real consequences. There's a new class of problems, where seasoned directors' experiences managing and monetizing traditional assets just doesn't translate. It is a daunting task to keep up with the growth of new competitors, those who are as likely to come from adjacent sectors as they are from one's own industry, rapid-fire funding cycles in Silicon Valley and other technology hotbeds, the fluidity of technology, the digital experiences customers demand, and the rise of non-traditional risks. Many boards are left feeling outmatched and overwhelmed.

In order to serve as effective thought partners, boards must move beyond an arms-length relationship with digital issues. The Board members will need better knowledge about the technology environment, its potential

178

impact on different parts of the company and its value chain, and thus about how digital can undermine existing strategies and stimulate the need for new ones. They also need faster, more effective ways to engage the organization and operate as a governing body and, critically, new means of attracting digital talent. Indeed, some CEOs and board members we know argue that the far-reaching nature of today's digital disruptions—which can necessitate long-term business-model changes with large, short-term costs—means boards must view themselves as the ultimate catalysts for digital transformation efforts. Otherwise, CEOs may be tempted to pass on to their successors the tackling of digital challenges.

At the very least, top-management teams need their boards to serve as strong digital sparring partners when they consider difficult questions such as investments in experimental initiatives that could reshape markets, or even whether the company is in the right business for the digital age. Here are four guiding principles for boosting the odds that boards will provide the digital engagement companies so badly need.

Educate the Executives

Few boards have enough combined digital expertise to have meaningful digital conversations with senior management. The Digital directors were defined as non-executive board members who play a significant operating role within a digital company, play a primarily digital operating role within a traditional company, or have two or more nonexecutive board roles at digital companies. The solution isn't simply to recruit one or two directors from an influential technology company. For one thing, there aren't enough of them to go around. More to the point, digital is so far-reaching—think e-commerce, mobile, security, the Internet of Things (IoT), and big data—that the knowledge and experience needed goes beyond one or two tech-savvy people.

To address these challenges, the nominating committee of one board created a matrix of the customer, market, and digital skills it felt it required to guide its key businesses over the next five to ten years. Doing so prompted the committee to look beyond well-fished pools of talent like Internet pure plays and known digital leaders and instead to consider adjacent sectors and businesses that had undergone a significant digital transformation. The identification of strong new board members was one result. What's more, the process of reflecting quite specifically on the digital skills that were most relevant to individual business lines helped the board engage at a deeper level, raising its collective understanding of technology and generating more productive conversations with management.

Often, special subcommittees and advisory councils can also narrow the insights gap. Today, only about 5 percent of corporate boards in North America have technology committees. While the number is likely to grow considerably, tomorrow's committees may well look different from today's. For example, some boards have begun convening several subject-specific advisory councils on technology topics. At one consumer-products Company, the board created what it called an advisory "ecosystem"—with councils focused on technology, finance, and customer categories— that has provided powerful, contextual learning for members. After brainstorming how IoT-connected systems could reshape the consumer experience, for example, the technology council landed on a radical notion: What would happen if the company organized the business around spaces such as the home, the car, and the office rather than product lines? While the board had no set plans to impose the structure on management, simply exploring the possibilities with board members opened up fresh avenues of discussion with the executive team on new business partners, as well as new apps and operating systems.

Evolving business models

Many boards are not well equipped to fully understand the sources of upheaval pressuring their business models. Consider, for example, the design of satisfying, human-centered experiences: it's fundamental to digital competition. Yet few board members spend enough time exploring how their companies are reshaping and monitoring those experiences or reviewing management plans to improve them. One way to find out is by kicking the tires. At one global consumer company, for instance, some board members put beta versions of new digital products and apps through the paces to gauge whether their features are compelling and the interface is smooth. Those board members gain hands-on insights and management gets well-informed feedback.

Board members also should push executives to explore and describe the organization's stock of digital assets—data that are accumulating across businesses, the level of data-analytics prowess, and how managers are using both to glean insights. Most companies underappreciate the potential of pattern analysis, machine learning, and sophisticated analytics that can churn through terabytes of text, sound, images, and other data to produce well-targeted insights on everything from disease diagnoses to how prolonged drought conditions might affect an investment portfolio. Companies that best capture, process, and apply those insights stand to gain an edge.

The Digitization, meanwhile, is changing business models by removing cost and waste and by stepping up the organization's pace. Cheap, scalable automation and new, lightweight IT architectures provide digital attackers the means to strip overhead expenses and operate at a fraction of incumbents' costs. Boards must challenge executives to respond since traditional players' high costs and low levels of agility encourage players from adjacent sectors to set up online marketplaces, disrupt established distributor networks, and sell directly to their customers.

The board of one electronic-parts manufacturer, for example, realized it was at risk of losing a significant share of the company's customer base to a fast-growing, online industrial distributor unless it moved quickly to beef up its own direct e-commerce sales capabilities. The competitor was offering similar parts at lower prices, as well as offering more customer-friendly features such as instant online quotes and automated purchasing and inventory-management systems. That prompted the board to push the CEO, chief information officer, and others for metrics and reports that went beyond traditional peer comparisons. By looking closely at the cycle times and operating margins of digital leaders, boards can determine whether executives are aiming high enough and, if not, they can push back—for example, by not accepting run-of-the-mill cost cuts of 10 percent when their companies could capture new value of 50 percent or even more by meeting attackers head-on.

Develop a digital strategy

Today's strategic discussions with executives require a different rhythm, one that matches the quickening pace of disruption. A major cyber attack can erase a third of a company's share value in a day, and a digital foe can pull the rug out from a thriving product category in six months. In this environment, meeting once or twice a year to review strategy no longer works. Regular check-ins are necessary to help senior company leaders negotiate the tension between short-term pressures from the financial markets and the longer-term imperative to launch sometimes costly digital initiatives.

One company fashioned what the board called a "tight-loose" structure, blending its normal sequence of formal meetings and management reporting with new, informal methods. Some directors now work in a tag team with a particular function and business leader, with whom they have a natural affinity for business background and interests. These relationships have helped directors to better understand events at ground level and to see how the culture and operating style is evolving with the company's digital strategy. Over time, such understanding has also generated greater board-level visibility into areas where digitization could yield new strategic value, while putting the board on the more solid footing in communicating new direction and initiatives to shareholders and analysts.

Boardroom dialogue shifts considerably when corporate boards start asking management questions such as:

1. "What are the handfuls of signals that tell you that an innovation is catching on with customers? And

2. How will you ramp up customer adoption and decrease the cost of customer acquisition when that happens?"

By encouraging such discussions, boards clarify their expectations about what kind of cultural change is required and reduce the hand-wringing that often stalls digital transformation in established businesses. Such dialogue also can instill a sense of urgency as managers seek to answer tough questions through rapid idea iteration and input gathering from customers, which board members with diverse experiences can help interpret. At a consumer-products company, one director engages with sales and marketing executives monthly to check their progress against detailed key performance indicators (KPIs) that measure how fast a key customer's segments are shifting to the company's digital channels.

Risk discussions need rethinking, too. Disturbingly, in an era of continual cyber threats, only about one in five directors in our experience feels confident that the necessary controls, metrics, and reporting are in place to address hacker incursions. One board subcommittee conducted an intensive daylong session with the company's IT leadership to define an acceptable risk appetite for the organization. Using survey data, it discovered that anything beyond two minutes of customer downtime each month would significantly erode customer confidence. The board charged IT with developing better resilience and response strategies to stay within the threshold.

The usage of robust tech tools, meanwhile, can help some directors get a better read on how to confront mounting marketplace risks arising from digital players. At one global bank, the board uses a digital dashboard that provides ready access to ten key operational KPIs, showing, for example, the percentage of the bank's daily service transactions that are performed without human interaction. The dashboard provides important markers (beyond standard financial metrics) for directors to measure progress toward the digitized delivery of banking services often provided by emerging competitors.

Digital Organization

In the push to enrich their ranks with tech talent, boards inevitably find that many digital directors are younger, have grown up in quite different organizational cultures, and may not have had much or even any board experience prior to their appointment. To ensure a good fit, searches must go beyond background and skills to encompass candidates' temperament and ability to commit time. The latter is critical when board members are increasingly devoting two to three days a month of work, plus extra hours for conference calls, retreats, and other check-ins.

We have seen instances where companies choose as a board member a successful CEO from a digitally native company who thrives on chaos and plays the role of Guru. However, in a board meeting with ten other senior leaders, a strong suit in edginess rarely pays off. New digital directors have to be able to influence change in the culture of the board and play well with others. There are alternatives, though. If a promising candidate can't commit to a directorship or doesn't meet all the board's requirements, an advisory role can still provide the board with valuable access to specialized expertise.

Induction and onboarding processes need to bridge the digital-traditional gap, as well. One board was thrilled to lock in the appointment of a rising tech star that held senior-leadership positions at a number of prominent digital companies. The board created a special onboarding program for her that was slightly longer than the typical onboarding process and delved into some topics in greater depth, such as the legal and fiduciary requirements that come with serving on a public board. Now that the induction period is over, she and the board chairman still meet monthly so she can share her perspectives and knowledge as a voice of the customer, and he can offer his institutional insights. The welcoming, collaborative approach has made it possible for the new director to be an effective board participant from the start.

Organizations also need to think ahead about how the digital competencies of new and existing directors will fit emerging strategies. One company determined that amassing substantial big data assets would be critical to its strategy and acquired a Silicon Valley big data business. The company's directors now attend sessions with the acquired company's management team, allowing them to get the grounding in big data and analytics. These insights have proven valuable in board discussions on digital investments and acquisition targets.

In summary, the board members need to increase their digital quotient if they hope to govern in a way that gets executives thinking beyond today's boundaries. Following the approaches we have outlined will no doubt put some new burdens on already stretched directors. However, the speed of digital progress confronting companies shows no sign of slowing, and the best boards will learn to engage executives more frequently, knowledgeable, and persuasively on the issues that matter most.

■ ■ ■

Chapter 9: Modernizing I.T for Digital Era

The objective of this chapter is to discuss the benefits of modernizing I.T landscape for Digital Era, which is imperative to any transformation project. This is the foundation of a new beginning. However, there are key risks and challenges that you'll face during this the transformation journey. This would help your organizations to prepare and transform your organization into the global Industry 4.0 standards.

As we discussed in the earlier chapters, going digital is not about implementing technology. It is based on the business outcomes and newer revenue model that is evolving. Indeed, the technology by platform for the digital era should be extensible, flexible to support the future business requirements. There may be requirements to expand channels of sales beyond the traditional channels. A lot of factors need to be analysed as part of the digital transformation strategy. Let's take the initial case study discussed earlier in the chapters. One of the large manufacturing companies in Europe has been running production operations using a legacy SAP ERP system (SAP R/3 4.6C) as on-premises solution. However, the company ran the organization-wide survey to consolidate feedback from the key is the ers by respective departments to arrive at come on grounds:

The following departments key users were surveyed as part of the key user survey conducted:

1. Finance & Controlling

a. Core finance, project costing & controlling

b. Digital invoice processing

2. Supply Chain

a. Supply Planning (Kinaxis tool)

3. Projects & Contracts

a. Project Contracts &

b.   Sales & Distribution

4.   Manufacturing

a.   Manufacturing Execution systems

The objectives of the survey conducted were to identify the key pain points across all domain areas. As a result of the survey, the discovery team identified common issues such as integration, lack of flexibility in analytics capabilities, too many production issues due to technical bugs causing productivity issues. Each department came up with the huge laundry list of issues, pain points to rectify and then wish list to improve.

Major User Pain points:

- Lack of easy to use features in the applications

- Lack of real-time data (OLAP) available for taking quick decisions

- Lack of flexibility in applications to extend customer requirements

- Lack of robust organization-wide reporting (analytics) and predictability capabilities

- Lack of intelligent capabilities such as the alert monitor to avert production issues etc.

- Integration issues leading to failures in scheduled jobs for data transfers

- Lack of integration with the plant real-time with sensors (IoT) etc.

- Increased Cycle time in month-end processing (Finance, Payroll activities)

- Labour intensive procurement activities such as Purchase request and Purchase Order PR/PO processes

- Lack of time for innovation and best practices implementation in business

- Lack of transparency

- Cost vs. benefits for implementing major quick wins. Often, these changes are managed via release management processes, hence it's time and cost consuming

- Increased IT investments without a return on investments (ROI) benefits

The IT discovery team identified many integration issues, data migration issues, system maintenance and cycle time for resolution of production issues as highlighted above. Mostly, business teams complained about the workflows, alerts that were not helpful in the current situation. If you look at the above case study, obviously the IT landscape needs to be transformed.

First, the teams worked on developing a high-level strategy to consolidate landscape for the business across all departments. Hence, the team identified quick wins such as standalone custom applications to retire and consolidate applications into one global landscape. We called it with a fancy name – 'Global Digital Manufacturing Landscape (GDML)', further, the technology evolved to support the GDML with a robust platform via the cloud. Indeed, a combination of the on-premises + cloud version.

The next level of IT integration evolved with the underlying platform encompassing hardware, software, dB layer and the application as highlighted below- simplified version:

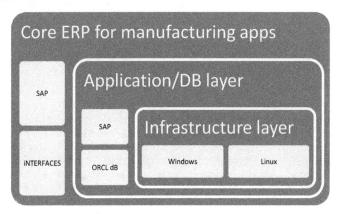

Figure 9-1 ERP Landscape

The landscape had transformed post digital transformation into just 2-in-a box, meaning just two layers. The first layer being the consumer, which is the business group and the second layer being the cloud provider taking out the complexities of windows/Linux and database activities as illustrated below:

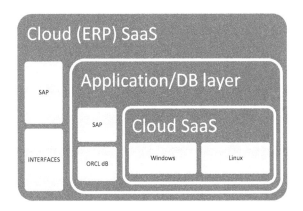

Figure 9-2 simplified cloud-based ERP layer

The above landscape eventually reduced IT spending by keeping the landscape lean with just two layers, one as cloud supported end-to-end by the partner and the business layer, which is the consumption layer. This is a remarkable development, as business had time and money to invest in innovation and rapid deployments of enhancements. This is just one part of the story with regard to simplification of IT; however, the major part was identifying the revenue streams.

The digital system scaled up with the required data for the end product maintenance and support services. The services stream became an additional revenue opportunity to resell digital software for maintenance, repair, and services due to investing in digital technologies. This system communicated between the train drivers and the back office to ensure the safety of passengers. This is a classic example of

Each of these departments had several customized applications with ERP as the common integrated system for supporting plants in production orders execution. Initially, these departments were following silo's approaches due to increased complexities. The support functions such as analytics (SAP BI/BO), SAP human resources (HR) and using third-party payroll interface applications that are critical to the core ERP. There were many regional applications for income tax return processing etc., interfacing with the core ERP functions. Eventually, the IT systems became overly complex and lost focus due to issues in the respective work stream.

Some of the key questions to ask are the following:

- What is the outcome and benefits to the organization?

- How does your customer feel about the digital experiences?

- How are you planning to modernize without impacting the current state of business

- Identifying disruptive areas with a mitigation plan to support BAU (business-as-usual) operations

- What are the additional revenue streams developed by digital transformation?

- Is your IT landscape scalable, flexible and highly secure?

Perhaps, for some of the end-product service depots may be non-traditional depots with on-call service centers to support customer requirements as part of regular maintenance or additional services to support. These are all additional revenue streams. One of the top companies was developing a unified system to build an alert communication system for train drivers.

Whenever there is a possible failure of the engine or any other part, it is predicted well in advance and advises to replace or service due by informing the nearest service stations. Apparently, this alert system became service revenue for the entire organization. More so, customers had a choice to procure beyond the extended warranty, which was a new service revenue stream for the manufacturing company. This is a classic example of realizing customer requirements with an outcome-based approach.

In order to achieve full benefits of digital transformation, your IT landscape must be lean and robust. This is the basic approach of creating a robust platform with fewer integration requirements. The second principle in my view is to isolate business from technology-related issues.

Going Digital? Simple, Modern and Secure IT Backbone

To compete in today's always-on digital world, all enterprises need a fast, efficient and extensible IT foundation. It must reduce complexity, enhance agility, be easier to manage, and enable more resilient and protected ways of working.

These companies are seeking an ideal mix of best practices, technologies and thinking to be truly digital, in every sector across the globe. Being digital, how¬ever, isn't as simple as purchasing a bespoke technology stack, laying out the piece parts, assembling them and voilà – a digital enterprise emerges. The drive to digital requires care¬ful planning and integration of an array of technologies and models. These range from social, mobile, analytics and cloud platforms, to instrumented devices on the network's edge – the so-called Internet of Things (IoT) – to accommodations for automated tools and artificial intelligence (AI) engines that power everything from chatbots and quality assur¬ance testing environments, through predictive analytics and machine learning systems.

Therefore, IT organizations will need an IT backbone that is agile, intelligent, resilient and able to accommodate the accelerating progression of digital technologies and tools that are on most companies' IT roadmaps, or could appear from left field at a moment's notice. With this backbone, businesses will be equipped to fend off the continuous threat of "born digital" competitors and defeat corporate saboteurs and fraudsters that seek to turn an enterprise's digital operational advantages into critical liabilities. Just as important, they will be positioned to take advantage of the vast opportunities on the horizon that arise from new digital business models.

To grow revenue, market share and profitability in today's digital world, businesses need to consider technology changes at every layer of the enterprise. This assessment begins with an overhaul of the user experience, leveraging digital tools such as natural language search and virtual or augmented reality to help customers choose the most appealing products and enable staff to support them. These changes ultimately ripple down to the business processes required to deliver these new experiences; the applications that manipulate the data underlying the processes; and the databases that store customer, product, and finan¬cial data.

These accelerating requirements have enabled IT organizations to transform their legacy sys¬tems with modern digital platforms. The piecemeal approach, unfortunately, has also added unnecessary complexity to their IT infrastructures. To get their houses in order, CIOs and IT organizations must adapt to changing needs with faster and more flexible delivery through techniques including agile development methodologies and DevOps, which is combining development and operations to speed new applications to market. They must scale their capacity and their spending as demand changes while protecting the organization against a rising volume and variety of threats that can cripple an organization in a highly public New York minute.

With so much changing so quickly and with so much at stake, it's no longer feasible for organizations to spend 80%, 70% or even 60% of their IT budgets on maintaining their legacy systems. Nor is it acceptable that every acquisition, reorganization, and strategic partnership require cumbersome changes in legacy systems and the painstaking creation of point-to-point interfaces among them. By simplifying, modernizing and securing the digital infrastructure is its three-fold answer to today's digital mandate.

The simplification unlocks value by creating a more efficient digital backbone, reducing the cost of providing current IT services and freeing scarce funds and skills to work on "change the business" initiatives.

The Modernization for digital era introduces newer (cloud-enabled) architectures and replaces point-to-point interfaces between silo systems with a services-based approach that makes it easier, faster and less expensive to create the unified experiences users demand.

Securing the infrastructure means making, establishing and maintaining a resil¬ient IT landscape that can fend off the new and unpredictable threats that come with digitization without breaking the bank. This white paper explains why it is essential to simplify, modernize and secure the organization's digital backbone and provides key recommendations for doing so. We end with a future vision of how effective IT landscapes will evolve, and detail the next-generation business opportunities they will enable.

Digital Systems & Technology

Everywhere senior business and IT managers are finding an increasingly complex competitive landscape. Businesses are selling more products and services in more markets, across more channels and supporting them in new and different ways while complying with ever-increasing regulatory requirements – many of which impose conflicting demands. Every one of these requirements – not to mention recurring reorganizations, mergers or acquisitions – can mean more technologies for the IT organization to support.

Adding to that the sprawl of systems most organizations have accumulated over the years and the pockets of non-standard, "legacy platforms" adopted to meet short-term needs. These have made it difficult for IT to effectively manage operations and meet service level agreements (SLAs). The result is an all too common situation in which IT is a challenge to maintain, rather than an enabler of digital business. The more platforms an organization must support, the higher it's training and licensing costs, the harder it is to change business processes, and the more likely it is that perfor¬mance, reliability or security will suffer.

A simplified digital backbone not only meets the perennial need for lower costs through reduced staffing needs and vendor consolidation; more strategically, it also enables a lean and flexible organization that can deliver innovative products and services more quickly and efficiently to drive business growth. These are traditional, incremental cost containment or process improvements aren't enough. To overcome complexity and drive value, IT organizations must achieve a step-change simplification through three critical efforts:

Reducing legacy debt, which is the ongoing work required to maintain, enhance, secure and update existing applications and platforms. Every time the business creates or acquires a new application or infrastructure component, it adds to this debt. Year after year, application by application, this raises the cost of maintaining existing systems, the risk they will fail or leak valuable data, and the cost, time and effort to adapt to change. Trimming this debt requires consolidation and rationalization. That means taking inventory of existing applications, platforms, and infrastructure, eliminating those that are not essential and upgrading aging platforms whose value doesn't justify their cost. It also requires inte¬grated services delivery to ensure efficiency, coordination, and control of the entire IT portfolio, as well as new methodologies such as DevOps to make it easier to quickly replace or enhance older applications.

Simplifying processes - This begins with process engineering, guided by a cross-enterprise IT process framework for better and more effective management of functions such as manage¬ment of service providers, Agile development, DevOps, and testing. Simplification is further driven by process automation using frameworks such as IT service management (ITSM) and robotic process automation. Such automation reduces the cost of configuring and managing IT systems while enhancing quality and productivity.

The Process governance ensures the ongoing benefits of process simplification through a central¬ized framework encompassing IT architecture and data and IT/business interfaces that ensure effective stakeholder management and delivers measurable results. This approach also creates a standardized process for sourcing and vendor governance while establishing joint business/ IT process improvement efforts. A simplified digital backbone not only meets the perennial need for lower costs through reduced staffing needs and vendor consolidation; more strategically, it also enables a lean and flexible organization that can deliver innovative products and services more quickly and efficiently to drive business growth.

Unified Communications Services

A major wireless provider reduced its total cost of ownership by 34% while improving service levels by streamlining what had been a combination of three outside service providers and its own 400-person support staff. We worked with the company to improve its service management model and consoli¬date to a sole provider of Level 2 support for more than 370 applications in 28 domains, including application enhancements, test environment support, and release testing. Among other benefits, this simplification prevented more than 2,000 service incidents in the first six months and improved the first-level resolution to 45% in the first five months. SLA performance improved significantly through a governance-driven operating model.

Facilitating business/IT alignment. This is the never-ending process of ensuring that the work (and budget) of the IT organization most effectively and efficiently support the needs of the busi¬ness. The alignment that is required can be achieved through business value management, which includes an articulation of its value and its ability to meet if not exceed SLAs. Doing this alerts business leader to how much they are paying, what they are paying for, and the value they are receiving to maximize the value of IT investments.

Once the business has decided which IT capabilities to invest in, real-time service intelligence gives business managers up-to-the-minute insights that connect real-time events with historical pat¬terns to automatically address problems or opportunities. Effective business/IT alignment also requires best practices in business-IT governance and effective portfolio management that (like an investor managing his assets) continually realigns spending based on the importance and performance of various IT assets. 6

Yet another tool is intelligent demand management, which aligns IT capabilities and business requirements by explaining the cost of various IT services, prioritizing those services based on their value, and working with the business to optimize spend. An effective program manage¬ment office (PMO) helps by mapping the IT portfolio with business needs, which keeps the business informed about the cost and value of various IT initiatives.

The result is improved alignment, faster and better decision making, improved customer satisfac¬tion through a clearer understanding of the value of IT investments, and the opportunity for IT to become a strategic partner to the business rather than providing "backroom" support services.

Modernizing IT with SMAC

Your IT landscape is evolving with the evolving cloud, mobile, social and analytic platforms, combined with the rise of micro-services, IoT and virtual and augmented reality, make for a dynamic and fluid IT landscape. These technologies enable the rise of digital business models while also enabling new customer services that can drive change in almost every business process across the organization.

Yet, too many organizations are stuck with an alphabet soup of inflexible, aging and poorly integrated systems that soak up resources while making it harder, not easier, to meet business goals. They also keep organizations mired in broken, inefficient processes that reduce employee productivity and cus¬tomer satisfaction.

There are many excuses for not modernizing the IT landscape due to fear of overspending in an uncertain or sluggish economy to not knowing where to start, to the difficulty of measuring the value of existing applications, to lack of top management support. But, modernization is an imperative for competing in today's cus¬tomer-aware, hyper-personalized and always-on digital marketplace, in which customers expect products and service offer that are based on the digital trails2 they leave with every interaction.

Summary

In this chapter, you've studied the essentials of modernizing IT for Digital Era with core strategy discussed for transformation with case studies.

■ ■ ■

Chapter 10: Common Pitfalls

The objective of this chapter is to discuss common pitfalls of the Industry 4.0- Digital Transformation projects. It is important to understand and these pitfalls, in order to mitigate risk in a large enterprise-wide transformation journey. This would help your organizations to prepare and transform to the global Industry 4.0 standards. This is a top agenda in the heart of corporate strategy, however without appropriate planning; this may lead to a disaster.

Over a period of time, leaders have felt the need for transformation, however, without adequate preparation and planning, they cannot succeed in the endeavor. A digital transformation program is very complex by nature as it involves all departments with a holistic approach to succeed. It means that stakeholders involving customers, partners, suppliers, business functions must align with one vision to succeed in this complex transformation journey.

Now, let's try to understand the common pitfalls in the journey of transformation. As discussed in the earlier chapters, digital transformation involves people, process, and technologies. However, it's a daunting task to align all stakeholders in view of people, process, and technology. Now, let's examine the common pitfalls related to the people, which is the first pillar in the transformation journey.

People

- Lack of innovative mindset & change management a. It's important to develop an innovative mindset. Be it re-skill requirements or changing organization structure or creating new KPI's for a digital era.

- Lack of visionary leadership & customer centricity

  o A good vision is required and empowers employees to carry forward. It's important to be focused on customer experience, satisfaction

- Lack of digital strategy & roadmap

  o Building a long-term roadmap and strategy of transformation is important to look ahead and plan for the future

- Lack of right communication, leading to job loss fears in employees

  o If you do not communicate, then employees will feel intimidated. Hence, it is important to plan your communication across departments to align with all stakeholders

- Lack of monetary benefits to motivate employees to innovate

  o It helps to motivate digital skills by providing real monetary awards and benefits

- Lack of digital skill gap, leading to employees leaving the organization a. Perhaps you've required IT skill set, however without the digital upgrade to your employees, your skills will not be of much help. Hence, it is important to conduct re-certification programs to internally develop required digital skills

- Agile methods of working as a flexible team

  o Most of the companies still do believe in waterfall methods. It's time to build robust Agile/Scrum methods to

197

implement digital technologies for the digital era

- Lack of collaboration with partners / internal departments

  o Most of the companies have partners to implement a technology. It's important to discuss with the partners and internal departments to collaborate more frequently to ensure the digital transformation strategy is carried forward diligently

- Lack of digital KPI's to measure performance a. Last but not least, it's important to measure KPI's. Every monthly, you should take stock of the situation to ensure the successful transformation

One of the common pitfalls with regard to people is the resistance to change. These are a type of people, those who claim – 'my way is the super highway'. Unfortunately, this situation may occur with leadership, the right to change or employees. It's a direct failure with leadership resistance to change. However, for enabling change within employees, there is a huge cultural change required within the organization by motivating employees to innovate, think out of the box and be more open. The innovative and openness is a cultural transformation. I am sure companies can come-up with HR strategies to hire new talent, re-skill and promote the right talent to lead the change management.

You'll need to re-think the best HR strategy to revise the organizational culture, however, this change cannot happen overnight. It has to be planned and executed over a period of time. In order to foster the innovation mindset and agile, employees must be educated about the upcoming roadmap and the benefits to the organization. Also, leading by example, awards to the talent will help the employees to be part of the innovative culture, as employees are the main pillars of the organization, it is imperative to start the transformation with the employees. Then, you can infuse change with the partners and suppliers in order to adapt to the challenges. Your partners and suppliers must understand your organizational vision and support in the journey of transformation.

First, an initiative is required to create an incubation unit within the organization to analyze the scope of digitization, preparedness and gradually infuse the cultural transformation with the innovative mindset. The HR will be responsible for identifying the right organizational structure to fit the right people in the right place. Once you've done with mapping the new incubation unit, recruit or transfer people to the roles with defined responsibilities. You must ensure good leadership in place to drive the change management to re-skill people, internal transfers with proper Organization structure. Once your internal teams drive the change management practices, gradually departments can adapt to the changes.

I believe with diligent reskilling, talent and change management practices, you can mitigate risks. A good learning content management (LMS) systems regarding the digital vision and global changes, it is possible to infuse innovativeness, instead of creating fear within employees. A good vision statement, combined with an award for the digital initiatives can drive an organization miles into digital transformation. With the good leader, who is visionary, most of the people related challenges can be resolved. It's important to communicate the vision effectively to be able to scale up in the digital transformation with a clearly defined output of the transformation. Indeed, I'd advocate KPI's measure successful transformation milestones to achieve the desired outcomes.

Another major factor is the lack of communication between departments. I've observed in most of the companies, people do not often communicate in a transparent manner, leading to several issues during the project execution. For example, sourcing, quality, and finance departments must be aligned and in sync in terms of vendor payments. One of the escalations that I managed was related to the delayed vendor payments. Indeed, the primary reason was due to the quality/sourcing not approving the invoices on-time, thus leading to delays. When we further investigated the issues in ERP system, we found the sourcing had different condition (rules) records that weren't fulfilled, however quality was okay.

In the end, based on discussions and some deviation from the original set of rules, both 'Quality' and 'Sourcing' discussed and finally agreed to process the supplier invoices. Finally, the finance team was happy with the change, since the finance teams complained about the delays in vendor payments. This sort of issues can be resolved with the people communicating with each other freely to avoid issues.

Leadership

It is important to establish who is in charge. Digital transformation requires board-level support and effective communication. As a leader, you must emphasize the importance of top-down messaging driving engagement. People will either enable or disable change. On-site training support helps them adapt to new systems, but it is equally important to allow them time to see the benefits.

Now, let us explore common pitfalls related to the process, which is the second pillar of the transformation journey.

Process

1.   Digital transformation is not just automation

a.   Do not attempt to just automate processes in Silos. This may lead to disparate application landscape. It is important to develop a holistic roadmap of the end-to-end business processes with evolution. This will need to be supported by the IT evolution roadmap to fuel business growth

2.   Lack of end-to-end business process knowledge

a.   Often times, I have observed a lack of documentation/repository of end-to-end business processes such as Procure to pay, order to cash encompassing all applications and integration points. Therefore, you'll need two views in a box. View 1 - explaining the key e2e process with exploded application layer to get a holistic view of a business process and its underlying technology supporting the business

3.   Lack of end-to-end digital approach leading to silo's approach

a.   As stated above, you'll need a holistic vision to transform IT into a digital era.

4. Lack of process KPI's

a. Each of the above transformational work packages must be measured using KPI's/Department to ensure successful completion of milestones with tangible outcomes. I'd go over a milestone-based approach rather than the Big bang approach.

5. Lack of documented process and procedures a. You'll need to create the repository of the landscape including business process and application landscape

Well. You've embarked on the journey and stuck with most of the process related issues. As observed, one of the common pitfalls with digital transformation is mostly 'process' related. To be more specific, companies do automate several manual processes and claim it to be a digitally transformed organization. A big pitfall is the missed opportunity of simply trying to digitize traditional business models and processes.

One of the common pitfalls is the lack of holistic transformation approach without envisaging the big picture. Instead, departments take decisions individually to automate operations in silos. This is one of the major causes of failed programs. Indeed, I.T should assess organization-wide and scope the digital tasks by respective departments. End of the day, the digital transformation will impact everyone in the organization. It's not specific to I.T or the business; it's everyone in the organization. Hence, appropriate due diligence is required to ensure a successful transformation program.

Most companies look at how operational processes deliver value to the customer before selecting new systems, to ensure they are fit for purpose. You must use technology where it matters to drive efficiencies and accelerate change. The Transformational technology empowers businesses to look beyond current operations to a digital future.

If you're not able to drive additional revenue streams, then the real intent and value of digital transformation objectives are not achieved. One of the key opportunities of digital transformation is service-driven business models. For example, Amazon, Uber, Airbnb and other market disruptors used technology to reinvent the customer experience.

Based on the benchmark standards, process KPI's should be measured. You cannot claim departments as 'digitally transformed' without tangible outcomes. This is where KPI's dashboards will help in assessing the outcomes on a periodic basis.

Scope creep

We have noticed many large transformation projects fail due to a lack of strategic vision. This means defining at the outset what success looks like, which is outcome based approach by measuring KPI's. We've seen firms try to do too much at once and then go through a process of restructuring the initiative halfway through, wasting time and money. One of the main challenges is the ramping up big teams too quickly as you'd need to start small, think big, using small, dedicated teams and quick wins to prove the business case.

Now, let's explore common pitfalls related to technology, which is the third pillar of the transformation journey.

Technology

1.   Lack of awareness and selecting the right technology. It's not about the complex solution to implement.

a.   It can be a simple solution for complex business problems based on the need. For example. You may not need to replace legacy applications overnight. It can be an extension or a combination of on-premises + cloud. Perhaps, you can implement SaaS solutions on Cloud for new implementations, still utilizing the legacy applications. It depends on the strategy and evolution of the business model.

b.   There is no point in fancying space rocket technologies. To be precise, it is important to provide business outcomes by supporting the business leads. There is no point in implementing a complex solution for a simple business problem. For example, a local finance tool can probably do good accounting without having to build an ERP for regional accounting practices. However, it is important to ensure the tool is easy to use and self-sufficient for developing reports or back-end processing.

c.   Business team(s) should be able to find data as required. Also, the tool must be simple and easy for them, thus isolating complexities of hardware, software or customization. The business team anticipates the tool to be simple, easy to fetch required data and use! In the past, so many data warehouse tools had been developed with no major usage of these reporting applications.

2.   Lack of exploring new revenue models

a.   End of the day if IT evolution will need to support newer business models. We have seen many examples of new revenue streams developed by the business. Your IT landscape should fuel the innovation by the business. For example, Amazon, Uber are classic examples.

3.   Lack of technology platform to support the evolving business model

a.   A robust digital platform is imperative for the successful transformation. If you have disparate systems, it may lead to integration complexities. Thus, leading to issues in IT without being able to support the business.

Latest technology

Investing in the wrong technology is a major and expensive mistake. You must look at how operational processes deliver value to the customer before selecting new systems, to ensure they are fit for purpose. You should use technology where it matters to drive efficiencies and accelerate change as a principle. The Transformational technology empowers businesses to look beyond current operations to a digital future.

A big pitfall is the missed opportunity of simply trying to digitize traditional business models and processes. One of the key opportunities of digital transformation is the shift from product-driven business models to service-driven business models. For example, Amazon, Uber, Airbnb and other proved to be market disruptors by leveraging technology to reinvent the customer experience

Transforming into a digital enterprise can be a complicated process for businesses. This transformation will encourage users to use innovative business models and improves the experience of employees, customers, partners, and stakeholders through the use of technology. It's bringing together people, data and processes to create value for your customers and maintain a competitive advantage. Digital transformation can improve profitability, customer satisfaction and increase speed-to-market for any business.

However, many business owners are still slow to adopt digital technology because they are concerned about business process costs and focused on short-term revenues. The digital transformation is important to succeed. Your business can fully leverage the changes and opportunities of digital technologies today or miss out on the incredible value these tools present to businesses, both small and large scale. The real challenge for many businesses is not whether they should adopt current technology into their existing business processes. Rather, it's how to maximize digital technology without disrupting their existing business functions.

1.   What slows your business down?

2.   What roadblocks exist in your current processes that harm efficiency? For some, it's manual data entry. For example, I.T systems don't communicate with each other, so users are required to enter data into different areas. For others, it's a process bottleneck. One process goes through a single department and creates a bottleneck.

For instance, reporting still goes through the IT department in many businesses, creating delays. When you replace legacy processes with automated workflows and truly examine your current processes, you can reduce friction in the business processes and help users to innovate.

While the true objective of digital enterprise transformation is clear – the ability to deliver a unified, Omni-channel and, ideally, extraordinary customer experience – the goal is to attain a frictionless enterprise. In the past, friction was caused by time, distance and lack of information; technology has resolved that friction. To become frictionless today means disrupting the status quo, eliminating what exists by fostering a corporate culture that is aligned with customer-centric focus and core values. Perhaps, by redefining the business models to adapt to the changing marketplace. Every business wants its workforce to perform smarter, faster and more productively. Achieving that goal requires innovative solutions to make it easier for your employees to collaborate, communicate and exchange data without restrictions.

For example, the cloud productivity solutions like Microsoft Office 365 can help your staff work and collaborate at peak proficiency without wasting time by creating a more streamlined working environment. Office 365 features like Focused Inbox help you better focus on the emails that matter most to you. For example, Office 365 allows you to define specific teams and enable employees to collaborate easily, share calendars, exchange files and take and share notes using OneNote.

With increasing competition, it has become extremely important to encourage teamwork in the office. Working in teams enables employees to be quicker, more effective and deliver on tasks. Progressive companies are increasingly realizing the value of collaboration to ensure information doesn't remain in the silo.

On the flip side and one of the risks and challenges to tackle, as mentioned earlier: the more you automate, the less work for people, in theory. And the same goes for other mentioned benefits such as maintenance. The reason we mention it in the context of quality is that this is certainly one area where you see cobot popping up (cobot is a fancy term for advanced collaborative robots or put more simply: robots that fit collaboration between man and machine). Now, let us see the risks and challenges in the transformation journey.

However, the risk is that most of the leaders just automate a few processes with an end-to-end vision of a holistic digital transformation vision, thus leading manufacturers are poised to become disruptors. Still, things are changing and the main challenges to move towards the Industry 4.0 with Smart Manufacturing Initiatives Will Integrate IT and OT Systems to Achieve Advantages in Efficiency and Response Time. On top of challenges and opportunities regarding skill gaps, connected supply chains, real-time economy needs and uncertainties, caused by changing macroeconomic and geopolitical changes, ample challenges/opportunities exist to move beyond the mere optimization dimension and truly transform at the core with the customer and data taking center stage.

Be Realistic - Don't Call Out Digital Success Too Early!

Would you celebrate winning a gold medal before starting the race or winning the cricket test series before bowling a ball? Simply put, you wouldn't. When we look at digital transformation successes, it is very rare to find a company that is humble about its project wins and client successes, because market competition is making organizations hungry to win big, win more, and call out those wins. Success drives us to innovate more, not to shout about it. It's just who we are.

So when I think about big technology companies announcing digital wins, I wanted to truly understand what they were, why the cause for celebration? I suspected that often it's about creating a perception in the market about being a digital leader and that its often just digital wash. I dug a bit deeper and realized that the successes were premature to the whole digital transformation process and essentially, comparable to celebrating an Olympic medal 10 meters into the race. One company even went as far as saying that it had 'digitally-enabled' a bank's account application process when, in fact, all it had achieved was moving a few things online - but you still had the same security issues and transactional processes. We have delivered digital transformation at banks which has changed the entire way in which accounts are operated - such as enhancing security using Palm Vein biometrics (Palm Secure) on ATMs, therefore enhancing the customer experience.

Saying that you have digitalized through creating an online portal or setting up a new online process, does not mean you really have delivered a digital transformation. What are you going to do with the data that you're getting? How are you automating and analyzing that data? In the example of the bank, how have you digitally enabled the customer to deposit a cheque without coming into the bank? How will you ensure authentication and security has been done? How have you built-in mobility to these processes? In essence - what is the end-to-end digital transformation you want to achieve?

Take a holistic approach to your processes before you allow anyone to call it a success. But the most important factor is to be aware that when you do embark on a digital project, you will fail - but it's all about failing fast and failing forward.

Business transformation mistakes - integration

Most successful wholesale digital transformations are multi-vendor. That includes processes and people. The Digital transformation programs affect the whole value stream, so it's important to consider the upstream and downstream impact of changing one particular process. If you leave a gap in systems integration, people will find a manual workaround and this will compromise the outcomes. Many businesses place too much emphasis on systems implementation and too little on data quality and integration. In many cases the success of digital transformation initiatives has depended on setting the right expectations upfront, particularly around data transfer and conversion," he says.

Inconsistency

By 2020, 60% of digital transformation initiatives will not be able to scale up due to lack of strategic architecture or failure to back up customer experience with internal processes (IDC). This requires consistency across all channels. It's important to consider the entire chain of actions within the business that will impact the customer experience. Perhaps, you can have the best digital channel in the world, but if the execution does not enhance the customer experience, you will have failed to capitalize on the opportunity.

For example, a digital transformation from traditional stores to Omni-channel retail included the successful integration of physical and digital processes whereby customers and staff can access the online ordering system in-store. Following factors are critical for digital success:

1.   Innovation

Catapulting innovation to success

2.   Company Culture

Breaking the business mold

Too much focus on 'digital'

Digital transformation is about business transformation. Technology is simply the means to achieve this end. Despite this, many businesses expend nearly all of their effort on designing, building and funding technical solutions without spending time up front considering how the business plans to work differently as a result of using that technology.

If your plans for digital transformation don't start with a plan for how you are going to work differently then it's almost guaranteed that you won't. Sure your new platform might help you to make your existing ways of working more efficiently, but you're unlikely to maximize or even optimize the return on your investment. In order to get the real payoff, you need to plan what you'll need to change to really get the most out of your investment.

Too much focus on the 'project'

An over-focus on technology frequently leads to the second common pitfall - too much focus on 'the project'. The word itself suggests an activity with a defined start and end date. But a transformation to digital has no end date. It's a continuous and iterative process. A complete business case for digital transformation must consider not only what existing ways of working need to change, but also what new ways of working are going to be enabled through the digital investment. In other words, the creation of a new operating model.

Often this fundamental redesign of the operating model is overlooked because it is easier to justify the digital project on the basis of cost saving alone. Who doesn't like to save money? Existing costs are known and the new cost savings can be modeled against the investment. If the point of the business case is to get the project funded, surely that's enough, right?

Well, no. Although this approach helps to get 'the project' funded, the cost-saving case often doesn't place enough emphasis on what happens after 'the project' is closed down. In most cases that's actually where the savings, and even better, the revenue growth happens. So, if your business case lacks a wider context, the opportunity to make the real and lasting change and to generate really significant returns on your investment is lost.

208

There needs to be as much focus placed on the adoption of the technology as there is on the deployment. In many cases, the real missed opportunity in digital projects is in the failure of the business to adopt and adapt to the new capability that it delivers. You need to have a plan to reach beyond the project team and into the wider business to engage people in the transformation.

We call this the 'Realise' stage. It's where your investment begins to pay off. It's where your business moves from merely being proficient in operating your digital platform to the platform becoming integral to how your business behaves. It's about your business continually iterating to use your capability in new ways that were never even anticipated in your original business case. That's when you start seeing real returns.

Not enough focus on 'transformation'

Not every transformation project needs to be radical, but the fact is that if your business has recognized the need to transform, then you are probably doing it for the fundamental reasons. Usually, either, you believe there's an opportunity to grow revenue, exploit market opportunities and disrupt your competitors with a new approach that differentiates you, delivers more customer value or achieves a different price point

You are responding to pressure from competitors or new entrants that are threatening disruptive business models that will change the game. Perhaps it's a bit of both. Either way, there should be a business payoff beyond incrementally shaving cost from your existing model that will inevitably be accompanied by the transformation in both technology and operating models.

If you have done your job well in the 'Invest' and 'Realise' phases, you'll need to worry less about iteration and incremental improvements to your existing business model. That should now happen as part of your day to day business. Real transformative thinking comes when you are free to consider how you'll be able to leverage your investment and new ways of working and apply them to new products, markets or business models.

We call this the "Multiply" stage - it's where you take your business model and capabilities and apply them to new areas. It's why Amazon isn't just a book retailer anymore. It might seem a long way away from where you are today, but this thinking is what gives your transformation project context and motivation. The multiple stages are not where you'll eventually get to once you have all your ducks in a row; it's where the entire transformation process starts, not ends.

The multiple stages sets the future vision that galvanizes your business into action. It creates the context for the digital projects you plan to run to get you there, both in terms of technology implementation and adoption. Sure, things will change along the way, but without this vision, your projects can seem like a series of disconnected activities.

These are the common pitfalls that we see when it comes to digital transformation. Our Invest-Realise-Multiply model aims to help you navigate these pitfalls and set an actionable path towards realizing the true value of your digital transformation project. It isn't a sequential effort, all of these phases run in parallel. They continuously shape and inform each other. And when that happens, you'll know your digital transformation project is achieving real change and delivering a real return.

Summary

In this chapter, you've studied the common pitfalls in the Industry 4.0 - Digital Transformation journey. In the end, all of these experiences would help you succeed in the transformation programs by learning from the common pitfalls.

■　　■　　■

Conclusion

The future is moving towards the digital World based on various artifacts discussed through this book. Perhaps, you might observe autonomous factories managed by a few Engineers using mobile applications in a couple of years. For most of the organizations, 2020 vision is not to automate process; indeed, a goal for most of the Industry leaders is to transform to Industry 4.0 – Digital Transformation. A visionary Digital Leader will transform from the legacy automation to the Digital Transformation – Industry 4.0. If you're not part of the journey of the Digital Transformation, you'll become extinct.

You'll need to be smarter in adapting self to the upcoming Digital trends to lead you to the next gen Digital Leadership in respective Industries. This is a true revolution of Industry 4.0 – Digital Business Transformation. The journey of Digital Transformation has already begun.

The future strategy will be less labor intensive with more intelligent robots engaged in additive manufacturing. There are few countries like Japan, which has already pioneered robotics in manufacturing industries. If you've observed the TV serial of late 80's, you'd have seen a Japanese TV-serial, 'GIANT ROBOT'. In that serial, a boy controls the GIANT MACHINE with his watch. I use to wonder, how this watch can do such things. But it is no more a sci-fi or a fiction in the current generation, as you know a Digital watch can transform into the mobile application that can run the entire production in a factory or turn into a gadget used for home entertainment etc. It is possible now, using the technology as an enabler to achieve goals smarter.

Furthermore, it's amazing to read articles on countries such as the USA experimenting very complicated human surgeries performed by the hi-tech robots with limited supervision by neuroscientists and Doctors. Thus, the world is evolving into another dimension of the Digital World. The future gaming, learning, and education, entertainment Industries will transform into a Digital ecosystem with digital schools, universities, hospitals with animation tools, technologies that can help in Digital business transformation. Therefore, every sector is going through this transformation journey. The advent of driverless cars, trains is not a myth anymore and the entire train control systems can be managed offshore from anywhere, anytime.

On the other hand, enhanced customer satisfaction is the key thing by providing 'UX'- user experience and Design thinking. Therefore the reality of Digital transformation is blossoming into reality from the conceptual stage. As you'd realized, Google has transformed itself from a search engine into a plethora of products and services spanning across Digital platform, technologies, databases, cloud infrastructure and driverless cars using geospatial technology.

A decade ago Apple created I-store with less than a hundred apps with less than 1000 subscribers, today it has more than a million subscribers with over 1000 apps in the instore. Every organization is striving hard to claim its identity in the Digital space by transforming its products and services with strong leadership and a fundamental shift in the mindset. I can give you in numerous examples of organizations that had transformed itself into the digital space. For example, Tesla making electric cars was a myth a decade ago, which is a reality now.

I wouldn't be surprised with the refrigerator with IoT enabled sensors capability, replenishing with the stocks arriving from the nearest grocery store. I wouldn't be surprised with my car services done with IoT communicating with the nearest service center, as part of the scheduled maintenance. Every sector is going through these changes right now. It's evolving into a new digital era. The retail is expanding into the multitude of markets by seizing opportunities of rapid digitization. With the advent of advanced mobility platforms, you can run the entire enterprise or monitor entire factory operations or closing a sales order or even using the surveillance app to monitor plants etc. Therefore, it is right in saying that 'World has shrunk' in the hands of mobility and cloud platforms. If technology is harnessed properly, then it is possible to ride the wave of technology to provide the enhanced user experience.

Often time, companies do simply digitize their services and claim to have transformed to Digital Transformation. This is not real. End of the day, these companies would have lost time and money. When I was part of GE, I have realized the importance of customer satisfaction over a period of time. There are few parameters such as reducing defects and process optimization which are the primary goal for any organization. Hence, it is essential to study the current environment and then transform it to the next level of Digital transformation by seizing opportunities in process optimization, enhancing customer behavior and user experiences, and also support the internal employees to do it a lot smarter with an innovative mindset by using enablers such as technology. It means a lot as part of the organizational culture with the significant focus on six sigma strategies to evolve enhanced customer satisfaction. It is not just a tool, perhaps it was a wonderful strategy deployed by companies such as GE to transform the entire organizational culture with the six sigma strategies to improve customer satisfaction.

Bottom line, every department showcased top 3 things to improve based on the six sigma analysis of parts-per-million (ppm) approach to reducing defects is very effective in large-scale production units and helped in enhancing customer satisfaction, reduced defects overall with its products and services. These changes didn't happen overnight, perhaps, it was a journey of transformation.

Thus, GE has evolved to the next generation platform with its products and services by exceeding all benchmark standards with the technology and transition from traditional mindset to the innovative mindset with good leadership, driving the changes from top-down with a vision and goals to achieve a high-quality transformation. This is the magic; these organizations have set classic examples of its shift in focus from just doing it to doing it to perfection. Indeed, they have mastered the art of perfection by remaining focused on customer satisfaction.

Once upon a time, business as usual (BAU) was often considered as good enough. In a World, where everything is connected and performance is reaching perfection, there is a raging tornado of changes happening with the self-driving cars. What you'd thought as a Science fiction is a fact today. I have heard IBM Watson with cognitive capabilities can challenge any chess grand-master in the world. Thus, the first time in the history there is an "AI" platform created by IBM known as Watson, for transforming business and uncovers insights, engage in new ways, and make decisions with more confidence. You might have heard the Chabot's are customer friendly with cognitive capabilities to support customer inquiries. You got to realize the revolution of Digital business transformation has already begun as you can see the revolution happening right now with your eyes open and hear out with open ears.

The way we work will never be the same. The skills will change. This is the transformational history of the Digital change. Ultimately, disruption has become a norm and changes are inevitable for any organization. The game changers such as Quantum computing fuels big data and Internet of Things (IoT) fuels Artificial Intelligence.

The human traits such as Creativity, Imagination, and emotions are increasing in every field of design and development of new product innovation (NPI). These are irreplaceable with machines; however, machines can get quanta of human thinking and aid humans to go far beyond the frontiers in space. With over 3.5 Billion search/day in Google, Big data is evolving to the next cycle of evolution. The AI is helping you in self-driven cars and Virtual Reality is helping in a business simulation with enhanced user experiences.

You got to engage with what might be and not what it is. We need to go beyond data and insights. The future is about the business model by developing new eco-systems. The new way to work is to embrace technology and the bigger future lies in transcending. The digital transformation is the future. It is not just creating a website for your organization or marketing campaign in the social media network.

There is a host of differences between doing Digital to Digital Innovators. These Digital Innovators are winning by the new technology adoption. The Digital Transformation is the journey of Strategic, planned Organization changes. It starts by creating new methods with a fearless culture of innovation. It is adopted by technologists, executives.

Good Luck in your transformation journey!!!

■   ■   ■

www.ingramcontent.com/pod-product-compliance
Lightning Source LLC
LaVergne TN
LVHW092332060326
832902LV00008B/594